In this book you will read ho  beautiful woman, with a great family, ıat most people would die for, would

You will enjoy reading a lot of ......, and interesting stories in the book. Like when she almost burned the firehouse down that she worked at, or how she snuck into the 1980 Winter Olympic USA-Soviet Union hockey game, or while rescuing someone in a raging fire the woman she was rescuing said to her, "It's about time you fuckers got here." She also recounts how as Chief Financial Officer of American Ski Company, she helped to take them public on Wall Street.

Her memoir will make you think, laugh and maybe even cry. It might also leave you in amazement. You won't be bored while waiting for 66 years of her life to be told because her life hasn't been boring, but rather, very interesting. She would be hard pressed to not find something to write about in a career that included 60 jobs, occupations, businesses owned or management positions.

She tells of her life journey and eventually coming out as a trans-woman to friends and family. She speaks to the amazing acceptance she has been fortunate to receive and the hurtful rejection she's experienced. She hopes it will end your curiosity as to what being transgender is all about. This story describes her raw human emotions and what it is like to hide something about yourself from family and friends for 55 years and then finally telling everyone! It has been proven to her thru this journey that people can change and reach self-actualization. Her reality has helped her to develop a personal mission statement, which is: To educate and enlighten people about the trans community by setting a good example and do so, one person at a time.

She hopes that after you've read this book you will be able to say, "Cami, you succeeded."

KENAI AND MARK,
ENJOY THE BOOK , STAY
INSPIRED !

Cami

DO YOU KNOW WHO I ONCE WAS?

A story of an unlikely journey to become

one's true self!

Cami Richardson

Dedication

This book is dedicated to my amazingly accepting spouse of 26 years, Teri Cook. There are not many women in this world that are willing to stay in a long-term marriage when their husband comes out as a transgender woman, but she has, and I am extremely thankful for her love and commitment to our marriage. When she said during our wedding vows, "Till death to us part," she meant it. Thank You Teri. I Love You!

Foreword

Everyone has events or dates in their lives they will never forget. I remember exactly where I was when I learned of the Space Shuttle Challenger explosion. I remember where I was as I heard separately about each of the four 9/11 plane crashes. I also remember the news I heard on October 11, 2015. That's the day my brother Tom called and asked me, "Do you know what today is?" My first answer was "Lindsay's Birthday" (his daughter). "Well yes," he replied, but that's not what I was referring to. It's National Coming Out Day and I am calling to tell you that I am transgender." I'll never forget that date now!

It was a call I never expected to get from my 62-year-old brother--my good-looking, out-going, athletic, and charismatic brother is transgender...how is that possible? To say I was surprised is a bit of an understatement. Sure, we always said Tom was a little metrosexual, but this was shocking. Initially, I didn't even tell my husband Mike because I was still trying to understand the whole thing.

Just to be clear, I know numerous people who are lesbian, gay and transgender, many friends and some acquaintants. I do not have a problem with it at all. My struggle was with the fact that I didn't understand how someone who was 62 could suddenly come out with none of us knowing until now. I felt bad that he had gone through this for so long and we had not been there to support him. I spent a lot of time trying to understand this news. Eventually, I realized that I might never understand it, but I certainly could accept and embrace it and be there now.

Since we live so far apart, we didn't see each other very often, but I saw Tom in February and July of 2016 and it was easy to accept the news since he still looked, acted and sounded just like the older brother I had known all my life. But I would be lying if I said I wasn't nervous to meet "Cami," the female name he'd chosen, for the first time.

In September of 2016 Cami was coming to town for her high school reunion and was to stay at our house. The day she arrived it was just Cami and I at our house and we had an opportunity to sit down and talk; I quickly discovered that other than the way she looks, she is still the same person inside, still fun to be with, still out-going, but now she is the person she apparently always wanted to be.

It takes a lot of guts to come out as transgender at any age, let alone at 62, and I know that Cami faces tough questions, odd looks and even hatred on a regular basis. I am proud to have Cami as my sister and I am proud of all that she is doing for the LGBTQ+ community. I love you Cami, keep on living life as you want!

Your "baby" sister, Terry

Prologue

Like any other day, I wake up and one of the first things I do is put my bra on, like most women do. After breakfast, I do my makeup and try to make this 60ish year-old face look like that of a beautiful woman. I love the challenge of putting on makeup and admire my work when done. I spray on my Coco Mademoiselle fragrance by Chanel and delight in its smell and femininity. I will dress today in a classy sophisticated look the same way I have dressed almost every day since August 26th, 2016, when I came out as transgender full time. I present myself as female to the outside world without regret or fear, but with confidence and excitement. I have embraced my femininity and strive to always present myself as a dignified woman. This is my new world and I love everyday of it.

But it wasn't always that way. I was a successful guy, married to a beautiful woman with a great family, who had an amazing career and lived a life that most people would envy. Then, I came out as a transwoman at 63 years old, shocking family and friends.

I was always afraid to confront my reality. I thought there was something wrong with me. At times, when I was young, I thought I was a freak, but I could never ask anyone about it or tell anyone as I was too embarrassed. In those early days a boy dressing as a girl was unheard of. There was no expert to go to or talk to and to explain my odd behavior.

During three major and very different careers I managed to hide it from everyone until I finally told my spouse when I was 55. I then waited another 8 years to tell everyone else in my life. I waited a long time to live the life I wanted to and that is why I love everyday of it now.

But, how did I get to today? What led me to make such a dramatic and life altering change? I will share my journey with you and along the way you will read some interesting, funny, serious, unbelievable yet true stories about my life. So, let's start at the beginning………

Chapter 1

I was born on July 30, 1953 in Mt. Vernon, New York to Anita and Bill Richardson, the second born of four children they would have. My name was Thomas Michael Richardson and growing up would be known as Tommy. We lived a very typical, lower middle-class life in Poughkeepsie, New York. My parents raised us in an Irish/Italian Catholic household. We lived in a classic cape cod style house that was one of the first built in a new neighborhood that was being developed. They bought their one and only house for $10,600 in 1953, the year I was born. It was a growing community, as IBM's Main Plant in Poughkeepsie was located within walking distance. Mom and Dad had moved us to "upstate" some 60 miles north of New York City, leaving his Irish and her Italian families in Mt. Vernon, NY, which was a very difficult thing to do at that time. They saw a new future working for IBM and took the biggest risk they would ever take in their lives.

The most significant thing I remember from when I was a young kid was when my mother's mother passed away. She died of a heart attack. I came back home from babysitting at a neighbor to my mother in tears. She told me Grandma had died. It was my first experience with death. I was confused and heartbroken. She was the quintessential Italian immigrant grandmother. Her husband, my grandfather, passed away long before I was born, so I never met him. She always dressed in black, as if she was still in mourning over his death. She was overweight mainly because she loved to cook and eat. We loved her pasta sauce and a visit to her house for dinner was pure ecstasy.

We visited my grandparents often. I remember a car accident we got in once while visiting family in Mt. Vernon. We were t-boned at an intersection one Sunday afternoon. My two brothers, sister and I were all in the backseat. There was no such thing as seat belts back them. We got tossed around pretty good, but there were no serious injuries. It was the first time something scary and dangerous had happened to me. It wouldn't be the last it turns out.

We were a typical IBM family. The 50's, 60's and 70's were a great time to be raised. We didn't live extravagantly but we were comfortable. We had limited exposure to how others lived, so I thought everyone lived like us. I had two brothers and a sister, and the dinner table was always filled with chatter about our day's activities. Our neighborhood provided plenty of chances to do things. We played lots of sports out on the street and at the neighborhood school. We also played war and as expected, no one ever wanted to be the German soldier.

I wasn't totally naive to the bigger world around us. I vividly remember when President Kennedy ~~was assassinated~~ 's assassination. We were released from school early and I can remember my parents watching our black and white TV and crying. It was such a sad moment that even I, at the young age of 10, felt the pain.

I was always very industrious. My first job was a paperboy ~~servicing the neighborhood paper route~~ that I delivered daily. The paper was the Poughkeepsie Journal. I had around 55 customers at its peak. I made about $10 per week, which was good for someone that young in 1963. It taught me to be responsible every day. It was turned over to me from my older brother John. I would in turn pass it on to my younger brother Jim. It was in our family for 10 years or so. I always knew who the non-payers were ~~who were trying to stiff me as~~ when they didn't pay, it came out of my ~~pay~~ pocket

When I ~~was reaching~~ reached my teenage years, my parents agreed that I could ~~do some~~ babysit for neighbors, all of whom had kids and many under 10. I was a good babysitter and loved taking care of the kids. I was often scared at night being by myself but fought through it. I felt bad when I would fall asleep and be awakened by the parents coming home. I felt like I cheated them, but I took their money anyway. I was practicing being an entrepreneur.

Chapter 2

My father was William (Bill) Richardson. He grew up in the Bronx and eventually settled in Mt. Vernon, N.Y. He served in World War 2 with distinction. He was a toolmaker for Ward Leonard before he was hired by IBM in Poughkeepsie. He was a very devout Catholic and became a founding member of St. Martin DePorres parish, when the diocese decided that our old parish, St. Mary's in Wappinger Falls, grew too big and needed to be divided based on one's location. We wound up in the new parish, and it ultimately changed my parents lives significantly. He was a great provider, worked hard and ultimately received the President's Award from IBM in his later years, something as a family we all took pride in as they didn't give out many each year.

I remember vividly one of my proudest moments of him, which was when he bowled a 700 series (703) in his IBM bowling league. I happened to be there that night and recall all the other bowlers crowding around the lane he was bowling at and rooting him along. He needed to finish with 3 strikes in the 10th frame and did just that. The other bowlers clapped and cheered, and I was very proud of what he had accomplished.

He wasn't the most competitive person but enjoyed sports, both playing and watching. He was an average golfer and in his later years he took great pride in standing behind me when I was playing with him and watch me drive the ball from the tee box. He was originally a big fan of the New York Giants in baseball, but when the Giants left New York he became a die-hard New York Met fan until his death. We lived very close to the IBM Main plant in Poughkeepsie and he would often walk to and from work if my mother needed the car as we couldn't afford a second car. I never really knew what a toolmaker did, but I knew it was more than making a hammer or a screwdriver. Turns out he helped design and make machines and tools to be used for the assembly of typewriters and eventually large main frame computers, which were just in their infancy.

I can remember later in life, after he had read in the stock offering prospectus how much I earned in a fiscal year with American Ski Company as Chief Financial Officer for a public company, he commented, "Do you realize you made more in one year then I made in my entire career." I did some quick math and realized that was believable as his top salary was $10,600 per year at the end of his career. Yet, he still managed to keep us housed and comfortable, clothed and fed and going on a yearly vacation to a dude ranch in the Catskills.

I also remember him paying bills on Sunday nights and once a month he would write out a check for $25 to send to his parents back in Mt. Vernon, so they had some extra money. He was a wonderful example of what a parents-son relationship should be, both as a son to them and a parent to me.

He rarely drank, which was odd since he was Irish. By virtue of him working at IBM the entire family could belong to the amazing IBM country club within a mile of our house and that we used all the time. I recall it costing him $3.50 per family member for a year. We would walk there almost daily during the summer, but the amazing thing is that we had to cross a very busy Rt. 9 (aka South Road), to get there. Our parents and other neighborhood parents never gave a second thought to us crossing that very busy road. "Be careful crossing the road" was all we heard. Today, a parent would be put in jail for allowing that. How times have changed. The country club had it all. Big swimming pools, baseball fields and leagues, summer camps, Christmas parties, 18-hole golf course, indoors and outdoors basketball, bowling alley, 4th of July fireworks and much more. In my college years, I would wind up working there for 2 years, which I loved. I never realized how good we had it until much later in life. It was a blue-collar paradise. IBM was a model company back then and we were fortunate that he chose to move us upstate and take the job.

My life was very much shaped by our religion as well as my schooling. My dad was a good, honest man and the perfect role model for young kids, like us, growing up. The biggest compliment I can say about him is to say that I have always strived to be the kind of person my father was and can honestly say that I don't believe I have reached that goal yet, but I'm still trying and feel I'm getting there.

I remember once when he was very old and nearing death, and he and I were sitting downstairs in the family room he had built many years earlier. We were looking at old books and came upon a book on WW11. He was never one to talk about himself much, so I asked him what it was like to be in the war. He had never talked about his service and we were always led to believe he was just a supply man. He quietly told me that he had served in the South Pacific war, which I knew. He then went on to say he had served as a Ball Turret Gunner in the belly of a B-17 and served 19 missions. I was surprised that after all these years he told me this. I asked him if he had shot down other planes and he said he had. He said, "It was shoot them or be shot down." This experience explained a lot as he was a very religious man and I think he must have felt regret in doing so and took to his religion to make amends to his God. I would never be the person he was as I never served our country as he did so admirably. It turns out I wouldn't be the man he was either.

Chapter 3

My mother, Anita (DiNardo), was an Italian immigrant from San Nicandro, who came over on the "big boat" when she was 11. I took for granted for many years that immigrants would work so hard to get to America because they saw a better life. I can't imagine what it was like for someone that young to leave your home for the unknown. I think having some of her Italian blood had a positive impact on me in ways that would come out in later years.

Ironically, my mother and her sister arrived in New York City at Ellis Island on Thanksgiving Day. After clearing thru customs and immigration they went into the city for dinner with family. She once told us, "We couldn't believe how well the Americans ate and thought it would be like that every day." But it wasn't to be, and she lived the tough life of an Italian immigrant growing up in Mt. Vernon, New York, mostly in poverty, but thankful to be in America.

She was a great mom, cook, housewife, friend and spouse. She wasn't the most educated woman, but considering she came to America speaking Italian, she did well. She had a bit of a temper when I know rubbed off on me, which to this day is my biggest challenge to keep under control. As I look back on my mother, some might have thought she was tough, but she developed a great sense of humor that became obvious to us as we grew older and went back to visit her.

There was always an Anita story that gets a laugh. Like the time we were travelling with our cousins and Aunt Ida and Uncle Joe in Washington, D.C. It made for a very crowded station wagon with a total of 11 of us packed in. I can't even remember the seating arrangement, but we were stuffed into the car. As we approached an intersection out of the clear blue my mother screams out, "Watch it Bill, a cop!!!" Well, my father was startled and instinctively slammed on the brakes. We all went flying and again, those were the days before seat belts. It turns out it wasn't even a cop and even if there was, there was no reason to scream it out anyway, unless she had concerns about all of us being stuffed into the car, which was illegal. My father was not happy and yelled at her in front of all of us. Luckily no one got hurt.

There was another time when, once again, all 11 of us were on vacation at Jones Beach. We were sitting on our blankets when a lifeguard walked by carrying a large red octagon shaped sign. Well, my mother asks, "Is that one of those newfangled surfboards?" The lifeguard looked at her and replied, "No Mam, it's just a Stop sign some kids stole."

My mother was a very devout Catholic and insisted that we attend church on Sundays and all Holidays and go to confession on Saturdays. I never gave it a second thought. It's what we did. I was thrilled when I became an altar boy. I would help and participate on the alter for Masses, weddings, funerals, Holiday events and whatever. I liked doing it and kind of felt like I was on stage. It made my parents very proud and at times myself and both brothers would all be on the altar as altar boys. In retrospect, I'm happy to say that I was never sexually assaulted by any Priests. It was a natural that I would go to a catholic grade school starting in kindergarten. She always stuck to the rules of the church and, for example, we would never eat meat on Fridays, and we would likely have fish sticks or marinara pasta instead.

I can remember after doing something wrong, her whacking me with a wooden spoon, which if it broke made her even madder. Yes, we were spanked as a kid. At the time, it seemed deserved, so I didn't think about it as a "big deal". That's how we grew up and it was a very normal form of discipline. I always hoped for the best, which was that she wouldn't add, "Wait till I tell your father." When that would happen, you knew you were in trouble. I think knowing that worked for me as usually I wasn't stupid enough to do whatever I had done, a second time. As I got older and my mother got fed up with me breaking wooden spoons, she came up with a different form of punishment. My father had renovated our unfinished basement into a beautiful family room. It was nicely done with wood paneling, drop ceiling, bar area, which would later prove to be valuable in my senior year of high school, and a white tile floor. The floor was nice, but scuff marks from shoes would leave long black marks on the floor.

Tired of me breaking her wooden spoons, she determined my new form of punishment would be to clean the scuff marks off the floor. I had to use a Brillo pad and scrub them off while on my hands and knees. Now that was real punishment. When I finally realized that if I acted properly, I would still have to do the floor, I realized my mother was way smarter then I.

She was a great Mom. I loved her dearly. I learned much from her. I learned values and that family matters. I learned how to respect elders and how to be a good person and citizen. Her Italian heritage became part of me. Many of the customs of Italians I adopted. I was the dutiful son, but for many years I hid from her the big secret of me wearing her lingerie. I don't know if she would have understood as I certainly didn't.

I adopted many Italian customs

Mom died of Alzheimer's when she was 83 in 2015. At the end of her life she didn't know who I was. Ironically, I didn't know who I was either any longer. I was in therapy and looking for answers. I often wonder why I came out right after she died. Was I still hiding my femininity from her after all those years? What would she have said? Would she have been accepting? I would never know the answers but hope she would have been accepting.

I brought up the subject of acceptance up to my sister Terry when I first came out and she said, "Well, when Mom and Dad were older, they would invite Rachel and her wife over for dinner and she was transgender, so I think she would have accepted you." Rachel grew up across the street from my parents. At a young age Rachel was Richard. He was very smart and went to college, which was in itself a first for our neighborhood. When he came back from college Richard had transitioned to Rachel. It was the talk of the neighborhood. I was a teenager when it happened and recall wondering, "How can that happen?" I was curious but too young to put it all together. I would one day find out for myself.

Chapter 4

I was in the eighth grade at St. Mary's grade school in Wappingers Falls, N.Y. during the 1966-67 school year. The first time I went to Our Lady of Lourdes High School in Poughkeepsie was to attend a varsity basketball game in February while I was in the eight-grade. Lourdes was playing Poughkeepsie High School in a yearly rivalry basketball game. The players for Poughkeepsie's team were mostly black, much taller and quite simply, better athletes. The Johnson brothers, of which there were three, dominated the team and the game. They were tall, heavy and imposing to say the least. The players for Lourdes were all white, Catholics, much smaller and the only thing they had going for themselves was that they were scrappy. I was thrilled to be attending my first high school game.

One of the reasons I was anxious to go was that the deadline to apply to ~~attend~~ Lourdes was rapidly approaching and I was trying to decide if I would go to the Catholic high school or to the public high school Poughkeepsie. My older brother John didn't go to Lourdes ~~when he graduated grade school.~~ I was more of an athlete, having played CYO basketball and Little League baseball. I envisioned myself playing lots of sports in high school and Lourdes had great sports teams. My parents were pushing for me to go, despite the financial drain it would put on the family. They point blank said one night, "We really would like you to go if your accepted." I knew that public schools were part of what they paid their taxes for and that if you attended a Catholic school, you had a tuition to pay. Despite that, I never heard them talk about the cost. They wanted me to go.

Lourdes played in a small, bandbox gym. It seated 300 in one set of wooden stands ~~and~~ around the sidelines. The school was the original Poughkeepsie High School. The city built a new high school in 1958, so the Catholic Archdiocese bought the old high school and started the Catholic high school. It was a classic old four-story high school on a small piece of land in the center of the black section of Poughkeepsie.

The game was a thriller and unforgettable. I knew basketball well and was an above average CYO player, but I hadn't seen this type of basketball before, except on the TV on the pro level. The Lourdes coach was a loud, domineering man named Vince Dutkowski, who I eventually played for. He figured out that the only way for Lourdes to beat Poughkeepsie was to slow the ball down and ~~by~~ controlling the ball. They didn't push the ball downcourt at all. They would take shots every 5 minutes. They were patient and let the good shots come and then took advantage of them. The gym was electric, and I was in awe. The excitement by the fans was something I had never seen before. The players from Poughkeepsie were so frustrated by the pace of play. I didn't want the game to end. I thought to myself, "I can actually go here and maybe play in this game some year." The final score was 18-16 in favor of Lourdes. It was bedlam and crazy at the end. I was at the game with some other good friends from grade school, Marty Gaw and Mike Mitchell, who also were thinking of going to Lourdes. I left the game and emphatically told them, "I'm definitely coming here." Marty and Mike both agreed, and we all applied. I was accepted and started in the fall of 1967. My parents were very proud of me.

I often wondered what would have happened if they caught me dressed. Would they have told me I couldn't go if they found out about my dressing? I knew where my mother kept her intimates. I often wore my mother's stockings, underwear and bras. I couldn't explain why I did this, especially pre-pubescent. At eight years old, I wasn't experiencing an orgasm, which I didn't even have a clue about, but I still liked it. I felt like a girl when I dressed and didn't understand why I liked it or did it.

My parents were good Catholics but apparently missed the class on how to tell me and my siblings about the birds and the bees. As a freshman I started to have erections. I thought there was something wrong with me and thought, "What the hell is going on with me?" I was scared, but not enough to mention it to my parents. When I finally had a wet dream, I didn't know what to think. On one hand, it felt really good, but on the other, why would something this good be so scary to me? I thought I was dying of something. I soon learned that combining feminine dressing, with something that I would later learn was called masturbation, was worth the anxiety. I stopped feeling bad about it and thought it was normal. Of course, I never mentioned it to anyone and always did it behind closed doors. It was the start of a lifelong secret.

I was always hiding my dressing secret with great trepidation of being found out. I recall being so brazen that while in high school I bought a set of fake glue-on nails. I loved putting them on and seeing my fingers transform into women's. My favorite nails were French tips. Wearing them would often lead to me spending inordinate amounts of time in the bathroom, sometimes masturbating, which always got my parents or siblings mad. I don't know how often I would hear someone yelling, "Tommy, get out of the bathroom."

My mother was good at going through my things and would find stuff and ask me about it. I was always fearful she would find my fake nails if I kept them somewhere in my room. So, what did I do? I hid them in her cosmetic draw on the bottom under some of her other things. How stupid was that? To my knowledge, she never found them as she never mentioned it and I'm sure she would have. I don't know what I would have told her if she asked, so I'm glad she never asked. I managed to get through four years of high school and college without getting caught.

Although Lourdes was a co-ed school, the girls stayed on one side and the boys stayed on the other for classes. We did eat lunch together in the cafeteria, but there wasn't a lot of mingling going on during the school day for the first couple years. Serious interest in girls didn't really materialize until I was a junior. I had minor crushes, but none were serious. I had my own "thing" going on.

My freshman year was all I was hoping for. I got elected to the Student Council, ran cross-country to get in shape for basketball, where I played on the freshman team, and played baseball as well. I was a jock and mainly hung with my fellow teammates. I had a severe case of acne, which made me keenly aware of my appearance. I couldn't imagine any girl liking me with pimples all over my face.

Despite that, I liked hanging around with girls. I liked the way they looked dressed in their uniform, which was a plaid skirt with a white top and perhaps a blue sweater. It left a lot to the imagination, but mine was already filled with my own ideas of being feminine. The boys wore a sports coat, white shirt and tie and gray pants. I never looked at it as a burden as I knew those were the rules.

I was a good student, with good grades. I can't say that I ever felt pressure to do well, as it came naturally. I was very social and helped organize the Freshman Frolic, which was our first yearly "prom." I asked a girl to come with me and we had a wonderful time. My freshman year was an awakening and a balancing act. I was very active and felt accomplished.

During the summer of 1968 I went with my family to our annual summer vacation to the Catskill Mountains. Shapanack was a dude ranch with small cabins, a social hall with a bar and dining facility, and a barn that offered horseback rides. We went with a neighboring family, the Krieger's, who had kids, the same ages as us. My mother's sister, Aunt Ida, and her family also came with us and we were all one big happy family for that week. We swam, went horseback riding, played baseball, hung out in the game room and ate in the dining hall with an eat as much as you want menu. One year in a competition with my older brother John, Bob Krieger ate over one hundred cheese ravioli in one sitting.

While there that summer I met Madeline Iovino, an attractive dark-skinned Sicilian Italian. One evening during the weekly dance, I asked her to join me for a slow song, "A Whiter Shade of Pale by Procol Harum." I was nervous as hell but got my way through the dance without stepping on her toes. I will never forget the moment it ended. I gave her a quick kiss on the lips. It was magical and a first for me. I had just turned 15 and I had my first crush on a girl.

When the week was over Madeline and I went back to our homes, almost 100 miles apart. I would occasionally write her, and she would respond back, but the distance proved to be too much, and our summer fling would-be put-on hold till hopefully the next year.

To this day, my favorite song of all time remains "A Whiter Shade of Pale." When I hear it, it brings me back to a much different time. A time of learning and exploring feelings for girls while trying to understand why I had the desire to dress in female clothes. In retrospect, I wish I had talked to someone about my fetish. I thought there was something wrong with me, but the pleasure that came with it was an addiction that I didn't want to have end. Besides, who would I have told? I didn't even know what my fetish was called. The Catholic priest for our parish would have been a likely choice, but I was an altar boy and didn't think that he, Father Brinn, would let me continue if he heard something was that odd about me.

The secrecy of it all caused me to rethink a major career altering decision. I was a devout Catholic thanks to school and gave serious consideration to attending a Seminary. My parents loved the idea as to them this would be the ultimate. I wasn't so sure. I liked Lourdes but the cross-dressing thing was something that had a grip on me. I opted to not go.

Chapter 5

I met Lorraine Davies during my freshman year at Our Lady of Lourdes. We would often take the same bus shuttle over from Poughkeepsie High School to Lourdes in the morning. I can remember also sitting with her brother Mark, who was an upperclassman and on the golf team, but a nice enough guy that he would talk to me on the way over to the school. Lorraine was an active cheerleader during her time at Lourdes. I often saw her at games but never really looked at her as someone that I was interested in dating. We eventually became good friends in our senior year of high school and often hung around together.

We were in the same religious class and we once were part of a group going to the Jewish temple in Poughkeepsie to see what other religion's we're all about. In one of my most embarrassing moments she and I both started laughing uncontrollably while in the Temple, at the Rabbi. It didn't go unnoticed by the teachers and we were told to write an apology to the Rabbi of the Temple. We both knew we had done something wrong especially having been attending a Catholic High School. We were seniors and we were supposed to be class leaders and we made fools of ourselves. But ironically, it did bond us together, and our friendship continued to grow.

She was dating other classmen and always had an interest in a mutual friend Tim Murphy, who was a sports jock at our school. During the summer after graduation, Lorraine and I started dating on a more official basis. The problem was that she was going to go to college at Niagara University and attend the School of Nursing and I was going to stay in Poughkeepsie and attend Marist College and live at home. For the first time in a while we were going to be separated, but we made a pledge to continue to see each other.

I can remember my first trip to Niagara University with Tom Gyseck, Marty Gaw, Steve Franklin and myself. It was my first big road trip on my own. Niagara had separate dorms for men and women so there was never going to be an opportunity for her and I to stay together while we were visiting. I stayed with Tom Gyseck, who also attended Niagara. The weekend was a blast and of course turned into a drunken party. Steve Franklin woke up one night while in a drunken stupor and instead of going to the bathroom took a pee in Tom's room-mates closet. That didn't go over well, and we were forced to leave the dorm rather quickly, luckily without injury. Being with Lorraine that weekend only intensified the feelings I had for her. We visited Niagara Falls, which was amazing. I remember making out with her in the lobby of her dorm because I couldn't go up to her room and I wasn't embarrassed about it. I was deeply in love!

We continued to date in our freshman year of college and during the next summer we both got jobs at the IBM East Fishkill manufacturing plant on the second shift. Our jobs were so mundane. We were responsible to solder one wire to another wire on a chip board. We had a nightly quota and upon leaving would grab a bottle of wine or beer and go somewhere to make out in my car. It was a great summer and we fell in love. She decided to transfer to Adelphia University on Long Island, which would make her much closer to Poughkeepsie where I was. I would often drive to Adelphi to spend the weekend with her. We would crash together on her single bed and were madly in love.

While in college, I got lucky and was hired by IBM at the IBM Country Club, only a mile from my parents' house where I lived. It was a great job and I worked in the athletic office giving out basketballs, taking tennis reservations, running the bowling lanes and was given permission to do any studying for my college classes.

I asked Lorraine to marry me two years before we graduated from college and set a date in June 1975, right after we both graduated. She would eventually find work as a nurse at St. Luke's Hospital in Beacon, N.Y. I would have a more difficult time as IBM wasn't hiring, which was where my father and older brother John were working. It was expected by my parents that I would work there but they had a hiring freeze going on.

I applied to a CPA firm in Albany and was offered a position. I remember the call vividly. I was so excited to be getting an offer. The partner said, "We would like to start you off at $5,000 per year." I was shocked as I was already making more than that working part time at the IBM Country Club. He tried to sweeten the deal and said, "Last year prior we hired someone from Siena College, and he has been given a $1,000 increase after his first year." I was stunned. Four years of college for that offer. I didn't accept the offer and needed to hit the pavement and find a job.

I was hired by A B Dick Co., a mimeograph company in town as a salesperson. I hated it and when the opportunity to take the test for paid firefighter in Arlington Fire Department came up, I took the test and scored #1 and was hired.

Lorraine and I got married on June 14, 1975 and lived in a cute apartment off the South Road. We bought our first house on Mockingbird Lane in 1976, close to my parent's house. I vividly recall thinking that the price at $44,000 was a lot of money and wondered if we could we could afford the monthly mortgage of $400 per month. We bit the bullet and jumped in with both feet.

In October 1978, we had our first daughter, Erin Leigh, and were proud parents. I was still an active volunteer firefighter at Croft Corners and our social life revolved around softball games, parades, conventions, Many close friendships with fellow firefighters and their families were developed. In October 1980, we welcomed our second daughter, Lindsay Ann.

She was a nurse and I was a firefighter. Life was good, and we made good money. I loved being a firefighter and had some amazing experiences.

Chapter 6

In the fall of 1979, I read a newspaper article that the Lake Placid fire department was looking for volunteer firefighters to provide fire protection during the 1980 Winter Olympic games. I thought it was too good to be true, but I contacted the Chief of the Department who said, "it's for real and I am looking for two crews of nine to come up and work two different weeks during the Olympics". I jumped right on it and contacted a few of my close friends within the fire department at Arlington to see if they wanted to join me. The spots filled up quickly, although we all were still naïve as to what to expect. My firefighting crew included my lifelong friend, Scott Karn, his brother, Kevin Karn, Horst Grunow, Mike Hackett, Dave (O J) Walsh, Steve Diamond, Gary Schoessow and Eddie David.

Lake Placid was a few hours' drive from Poughkeepsie and the day finally arrived and off we went full of excitement. We had been able to check in with a crew my brother John had organized, so we sort of knew what to expect. We were stopped at the staging area outside of town, parked our car and after a bus ride got access into the Olympic area. We went to the official check in area in town. I can remember anxiously waiting to get our Green pass, which would give us access to the Olympic area and various Olympic events at no charge. We were amazed that we would be able to get into events for free. We were housed in a mobile home in a "trailer park," along with a bunch of other volunteer workers. They were new and habitable, but nothing great. It would be our home for nine days. The accommodations were bunk beds and we ate at the nearby Holiday Inn with other volunteers and athletes. We thought we were in heaven. We had the run of the town and could even use the shuttles that moved athletes around. We wound up only working three shifts over nine days, two of which were night shifts where we would watch Canadian television and the events live until we went to sleep. We never had any calls in the three shifts.

We worked one day shift at the main fire station in downtown Lake Placid right across from where the hockey games and figure skating events were being held. I can remember Vice President Walter Mondale came into town via the Main Street past the fire station, in a motorcade with lights and sirens blaring. He was there to open the Olympics. I was in awe.

During that day shift, in someone's infinite wisdom (and not mine), some of us decided to sit out front and rate women with placards as they went by on a scale of 1-10. We thought it was great fun until we got in trouble after it was reported to department officials. We also made *the New York Daily News* with a picture, which only served as evidence of our misbehavior. We were lucky they didn't kick us out.

My reflections on doing this as I look back, especially considering my transition in later years, was incredulous. A woman never should be treated as a sexual object. If it happened to me as a transwoman today, I would not be happy and likely would say or do something. 39 years later I apologize for an act that should have never happened. Although it was a different time back then, there are no excuses for stupidity. Sorry ladies!

We went to various events throughout the week, including the figure skating pair of Ty and Randy Babylonia, Phil Mahre's slalom ski racing bronze at Whiteface, as well as various speed skating events at the outdoor oval. It was thrilling to see Eric Heiden win three gold medals during the Olympics.

One day we were trying to flag down a shuttle to take us to watch Heiden compete, He was riding in the shuttle that we waived down. He rolled down the window and we asked for a ride not knowing at first who he was, but he said, "I have to get down to the oval right away before I'm late" and he zoomed off. We walked away in complete amazement. We had just met Eric Heiden! Glad we weren't the reason he was late. He was the true hero of the 1980 Winter Olympics winning all five Gold medals in Men's competition. Ironically, today he is a Doctor in Park City where I live. I look forward to the day I can meet him again in person and tell him the story.

Each night we would head down to Mirror Lake and watch him and other American athletes receive their medals. We listened to the National Anthem with immense pride each night. The ceremonies weren't quite what they are today. The most exciting thing was the green laser lighting that shot up into the sky. It was more of a big party and everyone was having fun. It was also very close to Main Street where all the bars were. I remember us all being in the Woodshed bar one night (it was "The Bar" to be at during the Olympics) before the awards. We met these attractive women, who had driven in from lower New York. We welcomed them to come with us, as most guys would and the next thing you know they took to us and wound up sitting on our shoulders to get a better view that night and partying the night away with us. It was a crazy night and with a good buzz going, I finally left the party and went back to the trailer to sleep.

A short time later, I heard this commotion and noise coming from the road. Sure enough, it was the rest of the crew walking home. They had invited those girls and more back to our place to "crash". Beds were a shortage, so it didn't take long for one girl to jump into my lower bunk bed. As she cozied up with me on this very small bed, I asked what any typical straight male would and said, "If you are going to sleep with me, at least tell me your name." We became fast friends but went right to sleep.

We often found ourselves walking around the Lake Placid town during the Olympics to take in the excitement. It was a spectacle I will never forget. Lots of activity, national colors and both US and foreigners waving flags. Shops of all sorts on the Main Street welcomed all. Trading pins was the rage and I took part as well building up a good selection.

The highlight for me came toward the end of the Olympics. The USA hockey team had won first and second round games and earned a head-to-head match against the Soviet Union, who basically had a professional team against our college filled team. Our team was selected and had played together for the first-time only months earlier.

The Soviet Union was not a friend of the United States in any way, shape or form and there was a real fear of them. Kind of like now! Safe to say, we didn't like them, and they didn't like us! This game would be the closest we would get to war since the Cuban missile crisis. This was looming as one of the biggest hockey games ever and we were clearly big underdogs.

As the game approached, we heard that our green volunteer passes that were good for any event would not work at that game. We found out that attending would require you to also have a special purple ticket, which you would need to get prior to the game. We checked to see if we could get one, but they wouldn't give us any. We also learned that if we went into the venue earlier in the day, they were giving out the purple ticket with admittance. So, we went to watch some practice ice skating, got a purple ticket and prepared for our big "break in" that night. Scott, Gary and I devised a plan on how to get in. The others wanted nothing to do with it, thinking it wouldn't work. We would we would outfit ourselves as firefighters in our blue shirt, tie, dress pants and dress hat. We even pretended that a microphone, that was attached to the shirt lapel and tucked into the shirt was from a fire radio, but we didn't even have radios. The cord went nowhere.

The three of us then went to the entry point looking sharp, dressed as professional firefighters and there to do our "job". We had our green pass and we had our purple pass. We were nervous but had nothing to lose. We stopped at the Pinkerton guard station and he asked, "What are you guys up to?" I told him, "We are on fire watch in section 32 and are headed into work." He fell hook, line and sinker and to our amazement, he let us by. We did the same thing another time on the second level and with no other checkpoints we wound up in the venue ready for the game.

The game was thrilling to say the least and going into the third period we were ahead. We had positioned ourselves behind the *Daily News* reporter area. I was a huge fan of the *Daily News* as my father always brought the paper home at night for us to read. We were hanging off the rafters to watch the game. It was thrilling, and a dream come true. At the start of the third period, a New York State trooper came up to us and asked us what we were doing. I gave him the line "We're on fire watch" and he just looked at us, rolled his eyes and said, "That's bullshit." We begged him to let us stay explaining we really were firefighters, yada, yada, yada. He let us stay and just advised us to stop hanging off the rafters. The game would be watched around the world by millions and to think, I was in the venue watching it live.

We all know the ending, which is that the USA beat the Soviet Union 4-3. It has been voted as the number one most thrilling sporting event ever. The last seconds of the game were incredible with a chill going up my spine that I can still feel to this day. Al Michael's famous line, "Do you believe in miracles?" still echoes in my memory, as it was a miracle to have been there. We all left the stadium screaming "USA, USA, USA" and congregated on the Main Street in Lake Placid and along with thousands of other proud Americans partied our asses off. I called my wife Lorraine from a pay phone and screamed in excitement "We won," but got in trouble for ruining the surprise as it wasn't shown live as it would be shown later that night on tape delay. Off to the Woodshed Bar we went. It was truly one of those nights that I will never, ever forget. It made you so proud to be an American. Every year around the anniversary date, I vividly recall that entire experience and think how lucky I was. The United States ultimately would go on to win the gold on Sunday, but most people only remember that Soviet Union showdown and think we won the gold then.

The entire Olympic experience was truly an amazing dream that came true. I still have a certificate hanging in my office that was signed by the President of the Winter Olympic Games. I didn't participate as an athlete, but I certainly did get to participate both as a volunteer and as a proud American.

Chapter 7

Over the course of my eight years as a paid firefighter and many others as a volunteer, it was natural that some amazing life and death situations occurred. One in particular stands out. It was July 1978 on a hot summer night. I responded to the call while off duty and at home. The Red Bull Motor Inn, which was a mile from my house, was on fire. Three rooms on the first floor were fully involved when I pulled up. We had occupants on the second floor that we heard were trapped by the fire below.

My brother John, who was Lieutenant of Croft Corners Fire Company at the time, ordered me and one other firefighter and good friend, Joe Tamney, to go up the stairs and attempt to rescue those trapped. We slid our Scott packs on and up we went, staying low to the ground and began the search down the hallway. It was smoky and hot, and I knew it could be only a matter of minutes before the floor would be engulfed in fire. It was a dangerous position to be in as we were right above the fire and didn't have a hose-line.

We had a rough idea where to go. Sure enough, we inspected a room and came upon a woman, who was literally tying bed sheets together to escape through the hotel windows in her room. I went up to her to get her to come with us. Her comment to me was, "It's about time you fuckers got here!" It wasn't quite the greeting that I expected. I said to her, "Well, you can stay and go down your way or come with us."

She opted to go with us and after backtracking down a hot, smoky hallway and staircase we got her out safely. I shared my oxygen from my breathing apparatus with her on the way out. Off she went to the hospital without even a Thank You. I always wondered if she ever realized that she was very close to death. I did get my first "Heroism Award" for this crazy rescue, which was something I could be proud of and still have it hanging in my office.

Chapter 8

Let me tell you about my life's most embarrassing moment or what I commonly call my 'burning down the house' story. I had been a volunteer firefighter with the Croft Corners Fire Company for about four years, as I went through college.

One night myself and another firefighter were in the Croft Corners firehouse as we were beginning a renovation to the ready room, which is where we waited for fire calls to come in and believe it or not, drink beer. Yup, $.25 for a Pabst Blue Ribbon right out of an old soda machine. Anytime, any day, we could drink beer. Can you imagine this happening in today's day and age?

There was an upstairs attic that we needed to empty, so we climbed up and began the process. We discovered a box with a bunch of old US flags that had flown proudly over the fire station for years. My fellow volunteer and friend, Bobby Cohn, said that we should throw them away to which I advised him that that was not the proper way to dispose of a flag, that we needed to properly burn them. So down we go with the flags and off to the back of the firehouse on the side of the building.

We grabbed a 55-gallon drum, put the flags in them and I attempted to light them. The flags were polyester, so that didn't work, so I said, "Let me go get a gas can from the ladder truck". I go, grab the gas can, walk out and begin to pour some gas into what I thought was a drum that had burned itself out. Instead, a flicker of flame remained, which when the gas was poured into it ignited and exploded, causing me to drop the gas can, which was open and pouring gas out of it, catching it on fire. It got ugly quick as the gas was rolling towards the side of the firehouse headed for the double door and was spreading quickly. I was lucky that I did not get burned in the explosion. I quickly ran into the firehouse, picked up the red phone, which was a direct line to headquarters, which is also where I worked, and told them to put in a first alarm for the firehouse. The firefighter on duty who answered was amazed and said, "The firehouse?" I responded with, "Yes, the firehouse is on fire!"

I quickly pulled out Engine 5 from the bay and drove it around to the side of the building where the fire had intensified. Bobby pulled a mattydale line off the top of the engine and I began to set the pump. This should be easy. Or maybe not? Turned out not. When the hose had been laid out and was ready to be charged with Bobby on the nozzle, I opened the pump valve, but instead of the water coming out of the hose, the hose coupling had unscrewed off the top of the engine and the water was now shooting a hundred feet in the air. What the fuck! I had never seen anything like this in all my years and never would again.

In the meantime, back in those days, to notify other firefighters about a fire and where to go, there was a large horn on top of the fire station, that would blow out a certain amount of blasts indicating what street the fire call was on. So here I am, water shooting a hundred feet in the air and all I can hear is this deafening horn going off and the fire raging. It was chaotic scene.

Also, other firefighters started to arrive and sure enough one of them who happened to be the Assistant Chief, Bruce Griffin, ran through the truck bays and into the back room and not knowing any better, opened the double doors to the outside, which is exactly where the fire was burning. Now, instead of it just being on the outside of the building, it was racing inside. Realizing the water was shooting a hundred feet in the air, I quickly closed the valve. We managed to pull another line, I reset the pump and with help from other arriving firefighters, we were able to put the fire out. The damage to the outside of the building was a large burn area and it did advance to the inside of the building, but nothing too serious.

However, what was damaged was my ego! I got a phone call on the red direct line from AFD headquarters from the then Chief, James Clayt Laffin. He had been chief of the Arlington Fire District for many years and oversaw the paid company as well as 4 volunteer companies. I'll never forget when I picked up the line and he barked at me "Richardson, I could fire you right now. What the fuck is going on down there"? I told him what happened, and he couldn't believe the story and said, "We'll talk more in the morning." I had been on the job for only 30 days or so and I knew I had created a big problem for myself. It was a restless night with little sleep. I can't think of too many firefighters that can add to their resume that they almost burned their firehouse down.

To make things even worse, I was on duty the next morning and relieved the crew that came down to assist in putting out the fire from headquarters. I'll never forget as I walked into the small kitchen, that could barely hold six people, all of them sitting around a table drinking coffee and when I walked in, they all just started clapping and yelling "Way to go rookie, that's a classic fuckup!" It was truly my most embarrassing moment. Luckily, the Chief, in reviewing the situation and seeing it was an "error in judgement," just gave me a verbal reprimand. I stayed away from flags for the longest time. After a while, it did become the running joke on me for many years. It was not a moment to be proud of.

A valuable lesson was learned here. Along the way in life we're going to make mistakes and have some humbling and vulnerable moments. It makes you a better person in some ways to have this happen early in your life, so that you can learn to deal with your mistakes, learn from them and move on.

Chapter 9

One Saturday afternoon the fire company was hosting a fundraiser and we were cooking food and serving drinks, including beer, at the Oakwood Friends School where they were holding a big outdoor arts festival. After a couple of hours, a call for our ambulance came in for a woman in child labor a couple miles away. Our ambulance was stationed at the event and my brother, who was the Captain at the time, directed me to go with one other person. I had been a paid firefighter for a while at this point, but still volunteered at Croft. He trusted me and always seemed to volunteer me for calls.

In retrospect, I'm not sure why he didn't send at least one other person, if not two, as they were available. We got to the house and I went in to check on the woman, who was 31 and in labor with her third child with contractions every three to four minutes apart. Vitals all seemed normal. It didn't appear to me that we would have any issues getting her to the hospital, so we loaded her up on the stretcher and off we went in our old red Cadillac Station Wagon that had been converted into an ambulance.

I vividly recall calling in from the ambulance on the phone radio to Vassar hospital and very calmly saying, "Arlington ambulance 2 is proceeding in with a 31-year old woman, blood pressure is 116 over 71, contractions are three to four minutes apart. We will be there within 10 minutes." They responded, "10-4 Ambulance 2, we will be awaiting your arrival." It was common procedure that if you were headed to the hospital with an OBGYN emergency and the woman started to deliver the baby you were to pull over and deliver the baby off the side of the road.

About halfway to the hospital, we were driving north on South Road by the IBM main plant when the woman looked at me and screamed, "I need to deliver this baby right now," which wasn't what I expected or wanted to hear. My first thought was to put my leg between her crotch and just stop this from happening, but that wasn't part of the protocol. So, I took a deep breath and took action.

Now, all the training in the world never gets you prepared for the moment when it is time to deliver a baby in the back of an ambulance going 60 miles per hour by yourself. I got back on the radio and with my voice starting to get louder, I asked the hospital, "Should we continue in or pull over and deliver the baby now? We are within two miles." Protocol said we should pull over. They made the decision and said, "If you are that close, keep heading in."

I was rather nervous at this point. I pulled out the OBGYN kit, which was set up with everything anyone would need to deliver a baby. While talking on the radio at a voice level that later was best described as screaming into the mic, this woman started delivering the baby and I was giving a blow by blow description to the hospital. On we went to the hospital at warp speed. With amazing ease, as it was her third child, she pushed a couple of times and out came the baby into my blanketed arms. I somehow clamped then cut the umbilical cord and suctioned out the baby's mouth. I swaddled the baby boy in a soft blanket. The baby was gooey and bloody, but alive and breathing and so was Mom. Amazingly, so was I! I would later realize what an accomplishment it was.

We backed into the ambulance bay at the hospital and the nurses and doctors on duty all were there to help open the back door and get the woman and the baby out. As the door opened, all the nurses and doctors started clapping and yelling, "Way to go Tom, first one isn't it?"

In a complete state of euphoria, the driver and I went back to where we were having the fundraising event. I saw my brother John and told him, "I just delivered a baby." He couldn't believe it as OBGYN calls come in all the time and they usually never resulted in the need to deliver a baby.

It had been many moments of fear, with me questioning whether what I had learned would result in success. It did, and I wound up delivering my first baby, (there would later be a second.). It was excitement like I'd never felt before. The mother unexpectedly called me the next day and said, "We are so thankful to you and have decided to name the baby Tommy, after you." I was surprised and elated. They were a Chinese family, so somewhere out there is now a man named Tommy Chong living his life, thanks to me.

Weeks later, the hospital staff got me a tape of the entire call from Dutchess County fire dispatch and played it back for me. I wish I still had it as it was a classic example of someone going from a sense of calm to complete panic. It reminds me of the day I told everyone I was transitioning.

Chapter 10

I caught a job, which is another term for a bad fire, one night while off duty in a neighborhood house that was the same type of home that my parents owned. My brother John, who was Captain of Croft Corners Fire Company, was on scene and told me to grab a hose line and advised me as to where the fire was. A volunteer and I made an internal attack with an inch and a half hose-line. We quickly dosed the fire and by all accounts it was a clean, fast knockdown and I could be proud of our work.

The next day a picture of me was in *the Poughkeepsie Journal*, taken by a local photographer and friend, Judy Weiner. It was of me taking oxygen from a tank after the fire. I was sweaty, dirty and obviously one might assume I had been working hard to extinguish the fire. Behind me in the picture was a typical road sign, very clearly visible, depicted directly over my head. It was a DEAD END sign.

It struck me immediately that there was a hidden message in that picture that I needed to heed. I loved being a firefighter, but I had been sitting on my business degree from Marist College and always felt I should pursue other options. For the first time, I felt like I was in a DEAD END career, but I was doing well and had become the Municipal Training Officer for Arlington. My future was bright in the fire service, but I was itching to do more.

I was confused. I was also finding myself wearing my wife's clothes more often. It comforted me despite being 180 degrees different from who I appeared to be, which was a rough and tough firefighter. I remember wearing a G-string and nylon hi-top socks on a night shift and hiding it from my crew in the bunkroom. I was that addicted.

When I was 30, I left my job at the Arlington fire district and resigned from being a volunteer at Croft Corners. It was quite the 10-year run and stands out as one of the best periods of my life. Lots of great friendships were made, great times were had, and fires fought.

I was fortunate to have a great paid career at Arlington Fire, even though it was only seven and a half years. I had become the municipal training officer for Arlington and later on when I moved to Vermont became a Vermont State Fire Instructor.

Chapter 11

Lorraine and I loved Vermont and skiing Killington and would go there often to our good friend's house in Mt. Holly, Vt. In 1982, we bought a beautiful building lot on Little Lake St. Catherine in Wells, Vt. and started to build a second home. Right around that time, I got a call from my good friend Rob Dunne. He told me that Killington Ski Resort was hiring for an Internal Auditor position. I was so naive that I had to look up what an internal auditor even did. I sent in my resume and a handwritten letter, applying for the position. That move would change my life forever. I got hired and I left the fire service to be an Internal Auditor for a whopping $13,000 per year. I had been making over $30,000 per year as a firefighter. I rationalized the move by thinking that our newly constructed house wouldn't have a mortgage. The job as it turns out it was a great training ground for future growth and management possibilities.

Lorraine was 100% behind quitting our jobs and moving to Vermont, which was a risky move for a couple of 30-year old's. We had been married about eight years and our relationship was becoming typical of a couple with two young kids and jobs and our love life had changed. It didn't help that my two daughters lived in our master bedroom at first as their rooms weren't finished on the second floor.

I hadn't stopped dressing and I occasionally would wear Lorraine's lingerie. I loved the femininity of it. I was always afraid of getting caught, so I was very careful when I did it. This went on for many years and I had deep feelings of guilt.

Life moved on and in the late 1980's we decided to build a beautiful new home in North Clarendon, Vermont, which was closer to work for both of us. I was climbing the ladder at Killington and she was working as a nurse at Rutland Regional Hospital. We had two great kids. Erin and Lindsay, and then something changed. We would argue, and it could be explosive on both our parts. I didn't like myself when we got to this point of communicating. Lorraine and I were having difficulties in our marriage and I can't pinpoint any one specific reason for the problems and eventual breakup, but money and debt issues were high on the list.

Another was that we had been together since 1971 either as a couple or married for total of 16 years and the magic was gone. Our sex life became a second thought. We had given birth to two beautiful girls, who were then 12 and 10 years old. We struggled with the decision, but we separated in late 1990.

We both needed a change and the separation was fairly amicable. When we told Erin and Lindsay it was one of the saddest moments of my life, as well as Lorraine's.

We sat them on our bed and told them, "Mommy and Daddy are splitting up." There are many phrases people have to say in life they really don't want to, and this is one of the most disappointing things anyone could say. I didn't have a lot of confidence that I could rebuild what I had. I had the option to move into a condominium at Killington that I co-owned with my brother Jim. It was heartbreaking and at the time I felt my future seemed very bleak. I had a good job but feared what a divorce would bring. My fears would be quickly extinguished.

Chapter 12

One busy, cold mid-winter Saturday morning I was standing in front of the ticket booth at Killington thinking I might be able to answer questions, give directions, etc. I would often hang out at the ticket booth to help a ticket seller if needed. As Controller, I was also the individual that set policies and insured they were being adhered to, including one that stipulated that ticket sellers should check for signatures on the buyer's credit cards and if absent, ask for proof that it was the buyers, which was easily accomplished by showing a driver's license.

I was close enough to one window to hear a transaction getting a little heated. What happened was that the seller noticed that for this one transaction the buyer hadn't signed the credit card, so she asked him to show proof it was him. He responded, "Well that would mean me going back to my car for ID, which is too far and what I don't want to do. Believe me, this card is mine." Upon his refusal she called me up to the window to help resolve the situation. I asked for the credit card and then looked at him and upon seeing the name on the card I told the seller to complete the transaction, which she did. When he left, she looked at me in amazement and said, "Tom, you write these policies and you just went against your own policy." I then explained, "Well, I looked at the name on the card and then I looked at the person. I noticed something that made it obvious to me that he was the legitimate owner."

"How's that?" she asked. I replied, "Well, his name was Edward Kennedy Jr. and I happen to know that he is more commonly known as 'Teddy Jr.' He is the son of Senator Ted Kennedy, and had his leg amputated after coming down with bone cancer at 16. Well, when I looked at him closely, it was obvious he only had one leg, so I was pretty sure it was him. Kind of like, if the shoe fits wear it." Proof that there are times it makes sense to go against rules. We both had a good laugh over it.

I was still working during the winter of 1990-91 at Killington. At that time, management personnel like myself were asked to take on a second role and I oversaw the Killington Base Lodge operations, so I spent a lot of mornings there making sure things were going as expected. I can recall the first time I saw this woman, who turned out to be my future wife, was at Mahogany Ridge and I do remember thinking "Wow, she is beautiful." Our eyes quickly met one day, but that was it.

Being separated, I was realizing that I needed to have a woman in my life. I noticed her pattern, which was to show up early to ski, but always by herself. I was fascinated by her. Her hair was dark with some silver streaking and she was strikingly beautiful and still is. She seemed to love skiing and skied most of the day. I wanted to meet her and since I was legally separated from my first wife, I set out to do so. I felt uncomfortable approaching her in the base lodge, but the opportunity finally arose one bluebird winter day.

I was out free skiing in Bear Mountain, wearing my red Killington jacket indicating that I was an employee. I saw her in the lift maze, a good thirty people in front of me. I set out to catch up with her and started to pass skiers ahead by saying that I was management and needed to get by. I just barely got on the lift with her and sat next to her, literally skiing onto the chair before it left the loading area. I was nervous but struck up a conversation and asked her where she was headed. She said the Needles Eye mountain area to which of course I said, "I'm going to Needles Eye as well." I took a few runs with her and we seemed to hit it off. She was a strong skier. We swapped some stories about ourselves. When I left, I told her I would see her around. I was smitten for sure. She was a registered nurse from Westchester County in New York. A fellow New Yorker, which was appealing to me.

These were the days before cell phones, so I really didn't have a way to reach out to her unless I ran into her, but I knew what car she drove. A sporty red Mazda X, which was easy to spot in the Killington parking lot. I would often drop her a note leaving it under the windshield wiper. I asked her to meet me one morning bright and early at Superstar for some ski runs. We both showed up, but the weather was horribly cold, icy and rainy. We took one run and it was crazy bad. We decided to quit. I wanted to spend time with her, so I suggested we take a drive to Lake Champlain in Burlington, Vermont, a two-hour drive. She agreed and off we went with me playing hooky from work.

We talked the entire time getting there and got to know one another better. She grew up in Yorktown, New York, which was about an hour from Poughkeepsie. She came from a good Catholic family. We appeared to have many things in common.

The sun came out just as we parked at the edge of the lake and it was beautiful. I immediately felt like I had met someone that I could see myself taking the next step with. The day ended with us going for pizza in Pittsford, Vt. It was a great date and I knew I wanted to see her more.

We continued to see each other, and I communicated often via my car notes, which often made me feel like I was stalking her. One night we went out dancing at the Wobbly Barn and Pickle Barrel, where I discovered she could really dance. We skied together as often as possible. Talking with her was easy and we shared the same interests, like food and skiing. She wasn't a golfer, but willing to learn.

She was in hot pursuit by at least one other guy from her area in New York. I was aware of him and did my best to win her over. I knew I didn't want to play the field, so after a couple of months, I told her I loved her. It was spring, and we were laying alongside a pond in Killington on a blanket when I told her for the first time. She said she was falling in love as well, but she had other suitors and insisted that if we were to pursue this love affair, I would have to act on my separation and finalize the divorce.

We had a very serious discussion about our future that included a conversation about having children of our own. I had a strong feeling that my two girls were enough for me and amazingly she felt that she didn't want kids either. She was 32 and loved her life, which included lots of vacations, skiing and beaching and her freedom. I was sold on her.

I immediately went to work to finalize the divorce. I had written our Stipulation and presented it to the judge in Rutland Court. I didn't have a lawyer and represented myself. The judge was floored that we both could agree on all points and quickly granted the divorce decree. He commented to the others, including the lawyers in the room, "There is a lesson here for all of you. A divorce can be done without fighting and lawyers." It made me happy in many ways.

I had moved into my condo and she started to stay with me when she was at Killington. I so looked forward to her coming up and our sex life was very active. When the ski season ended, our relationship didn't. I would travel down to New York to her condo in Peekskill. It was a large, one bedroom that she had bought on her own a few years prior. She had a lot of flexibility in her scheduling that allowed her to create long stretches of time off. She would come and stay with me when she could.

She had rented an apartment in Newport Beach that summer with some of her close girlfriends, so she and I would often go down there for weekends. She looked just like Judith Light, the actress, and would often get mistaken for her. I had truly landed on my feet. I remember asking her to marry me while on a beach in Newport. I didn't think I would ever experience love again. She said yes, and our fairy tale romance would continue.

She would begin a crazy journey with me that began almost immediately. In mid-1991, I accepted a position at Loon Mountain in New Hampshire as the Treasurer/Director of Base Operations. We found a large condo in Woodstock, N.H. and settled in. My daughters, Erin and Lindsay, would come over every other weekend and we became one big happy family. Teri was still working in

Westchester, NY and would commute back and forth to cover her shifts. I would miss her terribly while she went back. We made new friends and I had met a great guy, Brian Ganey, who to this day is a great friend. In fact, he was our best man at our wedding at the top of Loon in March 1993. New Hampshire proved to be just a stopping point to what was ultimately to happen.

Following our wedding in March 1993 and after the ski season, the Loon Board had a meeting and made some significant cuts in staff and I was one of them. I was shocked, but realized I never really fit in there. The culture was different, and I was clearly an outsider. One morning in April, a few days before we were going on our honeymoon, I went in to work and was called into Sam Adam's office, the President, where he let me go and offered me a severance package. I embarrassingly went home to Teri, who was still asleep. I woke her to the news, and we cried together for the first time. I was vulnerable, humbled and scared. I immediately regretted leaving Killington, where I had been so comfortable in my job. We went on our honeymoon to Aruba anyway and talked about what our future might hold and where we would go.

Ironically, we were moving to another house rental and were packed to do so upon our return from our honeymoon. As fate would have it, I got a phone message from the hotel operator that Les Otten of Sunday River had called for me and wanted to speak with me. I was completely surprised, but the word had gotten out in the ski industry that I was available, and he remembered me from my Killington days. I quickly called him, and he told me he wanted to start buying other ski resorts and was interested in Wildcat in New Hampshire and needed my help. He immediately offered me a job as Vice President of Finance and I immediately accepted. I had landed back on my feet in a big way. Sunday River was becoming the ski resort in the East and was challenging Killington in all areas, especially being the first ski resort to open for the season. Teri and I set out on another journey, which would take us to Maine.

We took a ride to Bethel, Maine and started a search for a place to live. With some help from Les's real estate department, we found a spacious townhouse not far from the mountain. She decided the commute back to Westchester would be too long, so she left her RN position to live full time in Maine with me.

Teri accepted a position as the RN in charge of the base area ski patrol clinic. We worked near each other and it was fun. We would come home and swap work stories. She was a good clinical manager. She started the first drug testing process for ski area employment applicants in the country. I used to laugh upon seeing a potential employee read the sign saying they would be drug tested and watch them turn around and leave and never complete the application.

We were settling in nicely when an opportunity came up to buy one of my senior managers house, so we jumped all over it. It was on Songo Pond, just outside of Bethel proper. We loved the thought of living on the lake and soon after bought a small parcel of land right on the lake (we were across the road) that we renovated to include a little boat house for storage and a dock area. Of course, I had to have a speedboat, so I found one to purchase. Life was good, but about to change.

My youngest daughter, Lindsay, decided to attend Gould Academy in Bethel, Maine and would be moving in with Teri and me. I was excited that she wanted to live with us, and she moved in prior to her freshman year. Teri hadn't spent that much consistent time with her, so there would be an adjustment needed on everyone's part. I was working a lot and missed some of the interaction that was occurring, but like most teenagers, Lindsay wasn't easy to handle. She had a temper and mixed with my temper and with Teri in the background getting mad at me because of her, it got ugly at times.

For the first time in our marriage Teri was not happy. Lindsay and she clashed. Lindsay was not a very neat person and her room looked like a bomb landed. She was not always respectful to Teri, which was typical of a teenager. Teri was only her stepmother and I don't think they were on the same wavelength. It made for a difficult four years as I loved them both dearly and often felt split and could see both sides. The good news is that when Lindsay got married years later, she pulled Teri aside and told her how much she loved her and appreciated all she did for her and for putting up with her while at Gould Academy. It was very touching, and they have been close ever since.

Life has a funny way of acting itself out, but at the end of the day, love guides our actions. It took me awhile to realize how important family really is towards my mental and physical well-being, but now that I have and as I age, I appreciate family even more. I was blessed when my youngest daughter Lindsay and her family moved to Utah from Boston in 2018. I missed my oldest daughter Erin and her husband Greg, who were still back east in the Boston area. My parents have passed, but not some great memories of two beautiful people.

Our Maine journey was wonderful. Mainers are just plain good people. However, there was once when I got a speeding ticket driving to work one morning. I was speeding, so I deserved the ticket. The police officer didn't say much and was nice, or so I thought. I didn't mention it to Lindsay as it wasn't a big deal. One night she came back home telling us how the police officer was with her and a group of her friends and began bragging how he had given me a ticket. He knew I was someone important at Sunday River and thought it was cool. He didn't know that Lindsay was my daughter. She came home and told me the story laughing hysterical.

"Teri is cooking tonight." Those words, when spoken to friends or family bring immediate joy to them and me. We are both foodies and love good, different types of food and drink. When we first met, she won me over with her warm heart, personality, looks and her abilities as a chef.

For over 25 years, I have been treated almost daily to some of the most amazing 5-star dinners. Thank God for my daily morning walks with our dogs and being active in sports, which helps me keep my weight in check. She loves being in her kitchen and can spend the day puttering around, chopping veggies or making something yummy. She grew up in a mixed nationality family, but her mother was primarily Italian, and it rubbed off. I just love her meat sauce and have never tasted better. I have often thought that we should open-up a restaurant. She has always rejected the idea.

Chapter 13

In 1990, I was living in North Clarendon, Vermont with my wife Lorraine and two children in a beautiful new home that we recently had built and purchased. It was right near the Rutland County Airport and we often heard planes coming in and out.

One damp, foggy April Saturday morning I was headed out to the recycle center and as I was opening the garage door, I heard a very loud crash. It was a noise that I never heard before and it struck me as odd. I started off to the recycle center, but I kept thinking back to that noise. "What was that?" I thought. For whatever reason and more than likely simply fate, I said to myself, "I wonder if that was a plane crash?" I decided to go find out and drove quickly over to the airport entrance, which was only a mile away.

As I pulled into the parking lot of the terminal, a woman came screaming towards me frantically waving me down. She was hysterical and screaming, "My husband was flying in and I came to pick him up. I saw his plane crash into the woods on the far side of the runway." She pointed in the direction of the crash. The Rutland County Airport was not manned 24/7 and therefore no one was aware at this point of the crash. I asked her to go inside to make a call to the fire department and to get help.

Meanwhile, I drove onto and down the runway and headed to the far end of the airstrip where she had pointed to the approximate location. My heart was racing, and my adrenaline was flowing. I didn't know what to expect. I jumped out of the car and started to trudge through the wet and eerie forest. I was yelling loudly, "Hello, where are you, where are you?" There was no response. I could smell fuel. I went down one large hill and started up another and saw that the plane had landed amongst the trees. It was hanging precariously on tree limbs.

I reached the plane completely out of breath. I was somewhat skeptical of jumping into the cockpit. There was no fire, but I still smelled fuel. I quickly took sight of the pilot, who was still strapped in his seat and obviously hurt badly. I decided to take a chance and enter the plane and see what I could do to help him. My old firehouse EMT training came to the forefront. He was still conscious and could talk to me and was telling me where his injuries were, which included possible broken legs and arms and cuts all over. I took his vitals and they were ok, but not great. He was in shock and was screaming in pain. He mumbled for me to shut the power switch to the plane. I was nervous about flipping any switches but found the right one and took a chance. The power to the plane shut off and I felt a little safer from the leaking fuel. I tried to keep him awake and calm and was able to find a blanket in the cockpit to cover him, which kept him warm. I tried to extricate him the best I could while waiting for help, but he was trapped with his right foot stuck in the tight pilot seat area. I would need help and was excited to hear the sirens approaching. It seemed like an eternity before the fire department arrived on the scene, but it probably wasn't more than 15 minutes. With their help, we were able to extricate the pilot. He was in rough shape but would survive. We began the long difficult passage out to a waiting ambulance. It was back-breaking work for me and the rescue squad.

After he was on his way to the hospital, the Chief of the North Clarendon Fire Department came up to me and thanked me for my help. He knew I had prior fire department experience as had tried to recruit me when we first moved into the area. At that point in my life, I had had enough of being a firefighter and had told him, "No thanks, I am over that part of my life." I once again told him, "I am glad I could help on this incident, but I don't have any interest in joining the department." I drove home and walked into the house completely covered in dirt and blood and was all wet. My wife Lorraine looked at me and anxiously asked, "What the hell happened?" She had no idea of the crash until I told her the story.

It was a terrifying situation that I found myself in, but as I looked back on it, I felt I handled myself with calmness and efficiency. I had always reflected on my actions after my involvement in any rescue or fire scene. I could be very critical of myself and learned a lot by my mistakes. In this situation, what I had done, if I don't say for myself, was somewhat heroic. There wasn't ever any official recognition other than pictures that appeared of me in the Rutland Herald helping carry a stretcher with the guy on it and up the hill. I was proud of myself and what I had done at the scene. I am not sure if he was alive because of me or despite me, but he survived and that's all that mattered.

Chapter 14

One confusing result of dating and then marrying Teri was that I completely stopped dressing after I met her. I had been dressing a lot while still married to Lorraine, but I lost the desire when I found my new love. She was meeting all my feminine needs. She was sexy, beautiful and a woman's woman. When we would go out on dates, I watched her process to get ready and putting on her makeup carefully. I was envious as up to that point I had never used makeup as part of dressing up. I was living my femininity through her. I didn't miss dressing at all. I was concerned that someday she would find out and end our relationship. I would later find out in our relationship what kind of woman she really is. I went over ten years without even really thinking about dressing. I was so busy with my work career that I never gave it a second thought. I thought that I had beaten the addiction, but that would prove to not be the case.

In the mid 2000's I found myself going back to dressing. I would wear Teri's lingerie and clothes while home alone. It was a real turn on for me. I often felt complete panic when I was dressed and heard her or someone coming home early or without notice. My usual modus operandi was to have her call me when she was leaving work, so that I could change back to male clothes. I had started wearing make-up, which I would carefully put on and then make sure it was completely taken off.

I had a lot of guilt over dressing as I knew if caught it would be perceived as not only wrong, but very strange. But anyone fighting an addiction, like drugs or alcoholism, is fully aware that it can be difficult to stop. I was no different. I always wanted to stop and would go for brief periods without dressing, but then I would fall back into it.

Thanks to the internet I was reading and learning more about cross-dressing. I read that many men were dressing as women and that I was not alone. Like many, I would go for the sexy look with tight clothes, cleavage and heavy makeup. I would spend hours looking in the mirror and marveled at my appearance as a woman. I had become a narcissist. It was really confusing.

On a typical day I would dress up and then go for car rides, not putting my wig on till I was safely in the clear. I loved how I looked and thought I could "pass", which was my ultimate goal. I remember the first time I drove to Salt Lake City to go shopping after moving full time to the Park City area in 2008 and I was a nervous wreck. It was pretty obvious that I was a guy dressed as a girl, but I wanted to do it and didn't care what others thought. After a few times, I would confidently walk into a mall, with my heels clicking on the floor and felt euphoric. It was empowering and I truly didn't care what others were thinking. It was almost as if I was in a dream that had come true. I would occasionally get a positive comment from a salesclerk that would bolster my ego.

I started buying clothes at a rapid pace but kept them hidden from Teri. I was spending quite a bit of money, primarily at consignment shops. I kept this from Teri for a couple years without getting caught. I knew I was being deceitful, but I rationalized it by thinking it wasn't hurting her. I was so wrong. I was also slowly becoming more feminine. I shaved my body hair, wore clear nail polish, dyed my hair and was always tan. I felt happy and content and would stay that way until 2015 when Caitlyn Jenner introduced herself to the world and then my world would change dramatically. It was then that I decided I needed to get to the bottom of what was going on.

Chapter 15

As busy as I was with all our ski resort acquisitions, Les had placed me in charge of getting the Sunday River Golf Course started, which included negotiating a construction contract with Trent Jones Jr. a nationally famous golf course architect. He was a very smart guy and I was very impressed with his style and demeanor. I was proud to negotiate and sign a contract with him that he admitted was much lower than his normal pricing, but he really wanted to build this course in the mountains of Maine as he didn't have any courses in Maine.Trent and his team spent months studying and then drawing the site plans. He called me one day and said he was ready to make a presentation to us. Trent sent the plans to me in advance, so I could review them and show Les the drawings. As always, Les had his thoughts after I showed them to him. He had one idea that he thought was very cutting edge when he told me, although quite different then the norm.

On the day of the meeting Les and I met with Trent and one of his team members. I made the introductions in the conference room. In their respective sports, golf and skiing, both were industry leaders and well respected. It was cool to be able to finally have them meet and shake hands, not knowing what would result.

Trent started off with some pleasantries, but quickly got into explaining the drawings. Les was anxious to present his novel idea and within minutes interrupted Trent and said, "I wanted to throw an idea out here if you don't mind?" Trent reluctantly said, "Ok." Les continued, "What I hate about playing golf is getting stuck behind slow players and unable to play thru them. So, why not build a duplicate par 3 hole at the fourth hole? If a foursome wants to play thru, they ring a bell and are allowed to play the duplicate hole, so as to pass the foursome in front."

I was laughing inside thinking this response ought to be interesting. Well, Trent looked at Les and said, "Les, that's an interesting idea. In fact, my father tried that exact idea on a course in Chicago he built years ago, but it failed miserably. Now, let's get back to your drawings."

I had never seen Les put down like that before. Clearly, the golf guy knew more than the ski guy about the golf business. The course did finally get built and it is truly a place of beauty and I am proud to say I had something to do with it.

Chapter 16

By 1997, American Ski Company had become the largest owner of ski resorts in the country. In 5 years, we had purchased Killington, Mt. Snow, Sugarloaf, Attitash and Sugarbush in addition to starting with Sunday River in New England and Canyons, Steamboat and Heavenly out west. We were rolling and Les was crowned by the media as King of the Mountain. I was Senior Vice President and Chief Financial Officer and was living a dream.

Our ski resort acquisitions were setting us up to have to take the company public. Our need for capital to pay for resorts could not come from debt, as we were already
overleveraged, so we had to sell equity or stock in the company. This scared Les. He was used to being in charge and didn't like the idea of having a Board to report to and more importantly, not having 100% ownership. With no other options, we began the process to take ASC public immediately. We hired as our primary Securities firm Donaldson, Lufkin & Jenrette with help from Furman Selz, Morgan Stanley Dean Witter & Schroeder & Company Inc. These were all reputable Wall Street companies and since we were just a bunch of ski company guys, we definitely needed not only their help but their guidance.

We hired a financial consultant to assist us, who had become close friends with Les, our CEO. His name was Paul Wachter. He was an independent banker who specialized in helping Hospitality Resort companies like ours. He lived in New York, he was Jewish as was Les, he loved our story and we all hit it off pretty well. Chris Howard, who was now on our staff as our Chief Counsel would play an integral part in us going public. His legal background was just what we needed, and he could understand the big picture of what needed to happen and put the puzzle pieces together.

The process of going public is quite interesting. Ultimately, it comes down to trying to determine the correct valuation for the company. All factors are considered, including EBITDA (earnings before interest, taxes, depreciation and amortization), assets, liabilities and the net worth of the company.

One thing that was very clear was that Les wanted to maintain at least a 51% ownership, so as to still have voting control. 51% was not going to occur unless he went on the market and bought a bunch of shares himself. This became an interesting challenge as he needed to come up with some $20 million in order to do so. He certainly didn't have that laying around in cash, so the next best thing was his very lucrative family owned paintings by artists Van Gogh and Rembrandt that were in his mother's house in Teaneck, N.J. He was able to obtain a margin loan for the $20 million using the paintings as collateral. It would later turn out to be a big mistake when the stock price plummeted.

The Wall Street firms we hired all had a specific portion of the book to sell. They would go to their clients, tell them about the company and then give them a rough approximation of what the stock will go off at. It wasn't that easy a sale as we would be heavily in debt and dependent on growing EBITDA and Real Estate sales.

Les, Chris and I were all part of the 'Roadshow', which is where the executive management team and the bankers all begin to visit different cities in the US and Europe. The goal was to promote the company and its growth potential, so that stock can be sold. In the course of a day you might be flying to three or four different cities. Fortunately for us at that point we had leased a corporate jet that we were able to utilize even though it was expensive, but our time was precious, and it was more convenient. We didn't have to go through the public air terminal, and we would go to the private aviation companies to board our plane. It was a grueling schedule that lasted for the better part of a month. Lots of chicken dinners and presentations to investment groups. We did a tour of most major US cities, including New York, Boston, Pittsburg, Minneapolis, Atlanta, San Francisco and Los Angeles. The highlight was when we flew over to Europe in the Concorde supersonic jet. Meetings were scheduled for us in London, Paris, Brussels, Zurich, Amsterdam and Geneva.

Amsterdam was quite an experience. Our bankers from DLJ took us to a private club and it was quite the evening and one I'll never forget. I woke up with the worst hangover ever as did Les, who was not a big drinker. We were complete basket cases as we got into the limo to take us to Holland for another roadshow appearance. After we fell asleep in the backseat with our heads resting against one another the bankers took one look at our sad state of affairs and told the limo driver to take us back to the private airport. We took off for London and a return trip back to the States on the Concorde. It had been a world-wind excursion and a hard to forget experience in my life. Afterall, not everyone gets to take a company public.

Prior to the actual day of going public, I spent many, many hours and days with our lawyers, bankers and auditors in conference rooms in a high rise in New York City, writing, rewriting, editing and rewriting the prospectus. It needed to tell our complete story and needed to be completely accurate. I depended on two of my key guys, Chris Lavek and Dan Kashman, who were back in Maine at corporate headquarters to continually feed me the information we needed. They were consolidating all the financials of our nine ski resorts, which then had to then be audited by Price Waterhouse. The lead partner out of Boston for Price Waterhouse was a jovial, Irish guy named Jack McKinnon. He was a big Boston College and Notre Dame college sports fan. We got along great.

Wall Street bankers and corporate auditors were accustomed to doing this kind of tedious work. They had lower level financial analysts available to them 20 hours a day. After we would finally hit the sack, which was never early, those guys would continue to work into the wee hours. It was a grueling pace with constant demands, stress, long hours, switching of gears, eating poorly and the list just goes on and on. But it didn't take me long, based on my financial estimates, to realize what it would be worth to me on a personal level with all the shares I was going to be granted. There was an end game insight and I knew it. For years, Les had controlled the company in its entirety and I was now going to get "my share" for having helped grow it as big as it had become.

The big day finally arrived on November 6th, 1997. This was a big deal and my excitement level was high. With the help and support of many ASC staff members we even managed to bring a couple of truckloads of man-made snow down to Wall Street, and built a ski run right out in front of The Stock Exchange on Wall Street. Before the market opened, Les, Chris and I attended a breakfast in the New York Stockbrokers Club and became official lifetime members. We were treated like royalty, after all we were that day's Stock Exchange featured IPO company. We were interviewed by various Financial Networks and there was a lot of hope and optimism as the stock finally settled in at $18 per share. We had sold 14,750,000 shares of common stock on the NASDAQ Stock Exchange under the symbol SKI and had raised $265,500,000. I was going to receive grants of stock options for 100,334 shares of stock with an unexercised value of up to $2.8 million dollars.

My annual compensation that year was $170,000 and ultimately would quickly grow to $230,000 as CFO. I had become the Senior Vice President, Chief Financial Officer and Treasurer, as well as a Board member on the Board of Directors of a publicly traded company. Hard to believe for a guy that some 14 years earlier had been a paid firefighter in Poughkeepsie, N.Y. I knew he was very proud of me. Thank god he never found out I liked to dress up as a woman.   Dad?

After an initial surge that got the stock as high as $21 per share, we fell back by the end of the day. It was a fast-paced day. Unfortunately, I had to go downtown with Chris Howard right before the closing bell to deal with some problems with the rating agency, so I was not on the podium with Les when he closed out the day by ringing the bell on the stock exchange. I was a little bummed but considering how much money I had theoretically just earned; I could easily let it slide.

Les had come a long way in the ski industry and was now the King of the Mountain, but it didn't always look that he would be. His father was a wealthy German industrialist Jew at the start of WW2. At some point, he was arrested by the Nazis under Hitler's direction, but his lawyer was able to get him out on bond. He had over the years built up an amazing collection of original Rembrandts and Van Gogh oil paintings. He didn't want to leave them behind, so he cut them out of the frames, rolled them up and took them with him and he and his wife fled to Austria and escaped likely imprisonment and/or death. At some point, they immigrated over to Teaneck, New Jersey. For years, unbeknownst to others, that tiny home held some of the world's most priceless paintings by two of the world's most famous artists. It was a little unassuming Cape Cod house.

Les was born and raised in this small home in Teaneck, New Jersey. After graduating from Ithaca College, he started his career at Killington Ski Resort in the management trainee program. After showing some real potential, he was asked to go to Maine to Sunday River Ski Resort as asst. General Manager. Ultimately, in 1980 he wound up buying it from Ski Ltd. and at the age of 30, he wound up owning and operating a ski resort in Maine. His father never really liked the fact that he was in the ski industry. He thought that it was a waste of Les's time, and he would never make anything of it or himself. Les loved his father dearly, but he wasn't accepting any of his recommendations. He saw something that only driving entrepreneurs have a vision for and he would ultimately begin a journey that took him to Wall Street on this day.

We finished an exhausting day and flew back to Bethel, Maine in our privately-owned twin-engine turbo prop plane. Me, Les and the pilot Dan Bilodeau landed at the Bethel Airport on a quarter moon night. I'll never forget what then happened. Upon our landing and to my surprise, Les got off the plane and looked up into the moonlit sky and the eternal heavens and yelled, "Dad, look at me now," he exclaimed, "I'm worth 350 million dollars!!!!" Tears came to both our eyes and we hugged it out. His dreams had come true as had mine.

His words spoke volumes. In speaking to his dad that night, I think Les wanted to tell him that indeed he had made it and that his Dad could be very proud of his son at that moment. It was a moment that I will never forget. It was not only touching for him, but for me as well as it was the culmination of many years of hard work, and I knew I had helped make this happen for him. We were all driven to grow the company, sometimes blindly, yet with a passion most companies didn't have, which made up for our blindness. His favorite saying about staff was, "He/she just doesn't get it", or "He/she gets it." If you "got it" you were likely to stay for the ride. Obviously, I got it and what a ride it was.

I was appreciative to have been a part of this amazing experience. In my wildest dreams I would never have imagined that when I left the fire service, my life and career would turn out like it did. I was very proud of myself, as was Teri.

I was at the pinnacle of my work life and yet, I still questioned if I would go back to wearing women's clothes in private. It was driving me crazy that the hectic pace I was maintaining prohibited me from doing so. I had to put this desire aside until things settled down from a work perspective.

In my time as CFO I would help raise over $900 million in equity and debt for the company. Not bad for a guy that 15 years earlier was a paid firefighter. I was riding a wave that would soon come crashing down.

Chapter 17

Teri and I went out to a Board meeting in Lake Tahoe in the summer of 2018. Our stock price had dropped from the initial IPO price of $18 to around $12. Analysts were feeling the pressure to lower expectations as we were coming off a bad weather year and missed our hitting our numbers. In a private meeting of certain board members, it was discussed moving me out of the CFO position to a resort position and bring in someone with more public company experience. I couldn't disagree with the logic. In a series of senior management changes, I was moved to Managing Director of Sugarbush resort in Vermont. I had an amazing ride and although disappointed that I was leaving as CFO, I was going to a resort that I thought I could find independence and happiness in running.

Off to Sugarbush I went. I met my senior management staff and could see that me coming in after the popular managing director, Rich McGarry was transferred, wasn't going to be easy. Turns out that they weren't big fans of Les Otten nor the big corporate entity American Ski Company, all of which I represented. I could always sense that I was being talked about and not in a good way and in some cases being sabotaged.

At the start of my second ski season we opened early with a 3-foot storm in mid-November, that enabled us to open 2 weeks before Thanksgiving. There is an old saying in Vermont that goes, "Wait 5 minutes and the weather changes." Over the next 2 weeks it rained a lot and got warm and we had to close as the holiday weekend approached. I got a phone call from Les yelling at me for not figuring out how to stay open. He was being irrational, so I hung up on him. He called me back and fired me, saying that the managers there didn't like me. It was that quick. I had a panic attack, which scared those in the office, when I came running out of my office screaming in pain.

When I had a chance to reflect in the days that followed, I felt a true sense of relief. I accepted a termination package, so I would leave peacefully. I immediately cashed in my options, which I could now do, before the stock retreated any further. I cashed out at about $12/share and walked away with over $1.8 million. Almost all the other senior managers, who had options waited too late and most got nothing, like Les, who lost all $350 million he had theoretically made when we went public.

I started in June 1993 with Les and ended our relationship in November 1999. It was

an amazing 6 years and I achieved more than I could ever imagine. I wasn't sure what would happen next, but I felt I wanted to change things up. Teri and I were spending the winter of 1999-2000 at Sugarbush, but my termination made us rethink everything. We had recently renovated the house and enjoyed its newness, so we weren't in a great hurry, especially since I had cashed out my stock options.

Chapter 18

In early 2000, we talked about our options and we both seemed interested in owning and operating a Bed and Breakfast. We looked at one in Woodstock, Vt., but settled on a 15 room B&B on Martha's Vineyard called the Hanover House. We closed on April 30, 2000. We were so excited. I can remember Teri, while walking home from a closing dinner celebration on Main St. in Tisbury with our family, pulling me into a store alcove hugging me and saying ecstatically, "I can't believe we are living on Martha's Vineyard and own our own B&B." She was as happy as I have ever seen her. We ran it together and grew the business over the next 3 years. One moment I will never forget is when Teri and I watched the events of 9/11 in the office of the Inn. We hugged and cried together in complete amazement that this had happened to our country. We sold the Inn in 2003 for a nifty profit of over $1 million.

At one point in the 2000's Teri and I had so many things going it was insane. After we sold the B&B, we bought a successful garden/nursery center on Martha's Vineyard called Heather Gardens, which we owned from 2003 to 2008. I was also the managing partner of the Fairwinds Development project, where I built 12 affordable homes from 2001 to 2007. We also developed a Bead franchise in Sarasota, Fl. and then moved it to Park City from 2005-2011. We were also renovating and flipping houses in Sarasota, Florida at University Park Country Club from 2003-2008 and I was renting out our homes while not in them from 2003 to 2010. I was busy building modular homes on the Vineyard from 2005-2008, including our own new home and yet we still managed most weekends to have house guests.

I managed our business and household finances, which was quite a task. As I look back on this time, I once again was peaking in my business skills, except now it was for our own profit, not someone else. I won't lie, it was challenging and stressful. Money was going out fast and it seemed like it never came in fast enough. I did the books and the tax returns for all these businesses, which was mind blowing during tax season. I was juggling bank lines of credit, credit cards, vendors, politics and personalities and yet, at the end of the day (that now famous Wall Street saying), I believe I was successful.

Thank god for invention of cellphones as I was able to run all these businesses from wherever we were. My friends started to call me "'Telephone Tommy" as I was always on the phone. I loved the independence of being an entrepreneur. I was always busy. I can look back at this entrepreneurial timeframe with great pride. We were living an incredible lifestyle, but it was becoming clear to me that something had to give.

Over last 40 years I had a love affair with businesses and real estate. In fact, many family and friends would say I was 'addicted to the deal'. I had hits and I had misses. I like to remember the good ones, but it's hard to forget the bad ones. My partner in these deals was Teri, although occasionally I wondered off track and did deals with friends that I sometimes came to regret as something would inevitably get screwed up. I never lost a friendship because of it, but I know that uncomfortable feeling when your mad at a friend or they are mad at you. Unfortunately for me, when I get mad, I confront the person about it very quickly. In any case, I have done many real estate deals in my lifetime and I have opened my fair share of businesses.

Many of these real estate deals were in Florida and on Martha's Vineyard. We wound up buying our first Sarasota home in University Park in 2003. We found a small fixer upper with a cute courtyard and hot tub as well as a separate guest house. It needed cosmetic work, which both Teri and I enjoyed doing or coordinating. In short time, we had improved its appearance significantly and although our thought was not to do it to flip it, we recognized that the market was red hot and that we could make a quick $50k. So, we found another house that needed upgrading and sold the first one and rolled the profit into the second. We would then do a facelift, such as painting, flooring and cabinets.

Our intention was to keep this second one, as it was on the golf course in a nice community. A neighboring home went on the market, so we bought that one as well with intentions to fix it up, which we began. It didn't take long in the crazy real estate market that had developed in Florida for us to find another home that was bigger and better but didn't need any work. We cashed in on the other two, selling one to friends from Martha's Vineyard. We rolled all the profits into the newest house and like climbing a step ladder we wound up with a gorgeous home, but as it turns out a very hefty mortgage payment. We loved the University Park community and I became active in the HOA. We were active golfers and enjoyed the country club and its amenities, especially the Friday night socials

We were living the good life. We were the youngest couple in the development, for the most part, as I was around 50 and Teri was mid 40's. We got along great with our new friends and loved the Sarasota scene. We often ate at nice restaurants with our friends and went dancing at clubs. We belonged to the Country Club and became typical active members. We are both beach people, so many days we would be at Siesta Key or Lido Key beaches. We felt we had quasi-retired, although I always remained busy with my businesses and Teri still worked at Heather Gardens during the summer months, while we lived on the Vineyard. It was a good life as we also had bought a home in the Park City area and would rotate between all three.

Chapter 19

In the summer of 2001, a friend, Ed Herzeg approached me about joining in on an affordable housing development project in the Town of Tisbury that he and another one of his friends, Jim Stevenson, were beginning to start. It intrigued me for a number of reasons. It had enormous potential for income with not that much risk or cash outlay. If built, it would benefit those individuals that needed "affordable" housing, which covered the good feeling aspect. It also was very close to a lot that I had purchased and would be building a home on, so it wouldn't be a burden to get to. I wasn't so sure about the partners and what role we would take on. Since my specialty is finance, I was asked to handle the financial affairs. Ed was a relator, so he oversaw sales and Jim was to handle getting permits etc. He did the original work to find the opportunity.

The project involved a 14-acre parcel of land that had been deemed "undevelopable" due to zoning issues years prior. The homeowners around this land always felt it would be green space in perpetuity. However, in the state of Massachusetts, there was an affordable housing statute called "40B," which in effect, allowed these "undevelopable" parcels of land to be developed as long as certain "Affordable Housing" criteria were met and built. We knew it might present issues and could wind up being a protracted process, but we borrowed some bank money and with our sweat equity, we pressed on.

We had gone to Canada to check out modular home companies as that was how we would build the homes. I was driving and approached the Border crossing. The border agent asked, "Why are you guys coming into Canada." I said, "We are checking out modular home companies here as we are building an affordable housing project on Martha's Vineyard." He looked at us and said, "Affordable homes on Martha's Vineyard, know that's an oxymoron."

The local paper had written a somewhat biased story about our application, so the locals were fired up. We had asked for 32 homes to be built on the 12 acres. It would be cluster housing, with a mix of single family and townhomes that covered the low, mid and full price markets, which was required in the 40B application.

It was aggressive, and we found out quickly that getting all 32 units approved would not only be difficult, but impossible. Thy ordered the application to go before the Martha's Vineyard Commission, which was an approval board that handles special situations that might have an impact on the environment, traffic and character of Martha's Vineyard. Going through them was going to be another arduous process, with lots of meetings, legal bills, studies and headaches. They would eventually study every aspect of our project, from house design to road construction to planting of trees to block visibility. It was some pain in the ass and would take a year and a half.

As time dragged on, it became obvious to me and Ed that Jim was not going to be able to handle his responsibilities without our help, so I had to take on more. I became the defacto lead developer and did most of the presentations at these meetings. It is a good thing I did as I believe the Commission and the Board had confidence in me leading this project and living up to the restrictions and requirements. I had allies on the Board that supported affordable housing on the Vineyard, which had been a hot topic for years with very little to show for it. This development would be the first major affordable housing project on the Vineyard. At some point in this grueling process, the realities of making good money was overcome by the desire to get these homes approved for those who needed affordable housing. I was driven to get it approved and worked my ass off to do so. I had other business obligations going on, either the Bed and Breakfast or the garden/nursery, while working on getting approvals, so I was out straight for years. I loved every minute despite the stress.

Once again to relieve the stress, I found myself dressing more and more in secret. While Teri was out working, I would "work" from home, which included getting dressed up in her lingerie and clothes. I was always so embarrassed and fearful but enjoyed the feeling. Wearing stockings and a bra was a thrill. I needed and desired it.

I recall one day as I was dressed in a sexy red negligee, stockings and heels sitting boldly in my sunroom when a neighbor and her infant son came around the corner of the house headed towards the door. I quickly jumped up and ran to the bedroom. My heart was beating like crazy. I thought I had been outed. She was knocking on the door and yelling my name, "Tom, Tom." I'm pretty sure she had, at a minimum, seen me, just not sure what she saw. I never answered the door and she finally walked home. As scary as that was it didn't stop me from dressing again.

The approval process dragged on and on and rolled into a second year. It was going slow and I did my best to speed it along, but my hands were often tied while waiting on others and meetings to occur. After a grueling ordeal, that included the project being shrunk down on our part to 24 homes, then 16, and finally 14 units we got approval from the Martha's Vineyard Commission, but we then had to go back to the Zoning Board of Tisbury for their final approval. I did have an ally on the Board, a friend and fellow Bed and Breakfast owner, Jeff Kristal. He was fair and lived by the rules, which really made it hard for them not to approve the project as there was no legal reason not to. After over 2 years in the planning, we finally got approval in mid-2003 from the Zoning Board, where we eventually negotiated it down to twelve units in ten structures.

One of the highlights of the project after approval was the night that applicants for the affordable homes came together for a lottery drawing to determine who would get the low- and mid-income homes. When the winners were announced there was much excitement. I felt like I was truly helping those in need. I would work closely with these families in planning their new home. I did a good job for them, although in trying to protect the shrinking profits, I had to say No often.

The final project was to consist of four low-income houses, two mid-income houses and six full priced homes. The homes were not going to be stick built, but rather modular homes from Excel Homes in Pennsylvania. They would be trucked up in pieces to the barge site in New Bedford, Ma. They then would then be barged over to Vineyard Haven and to Packer's Warf. From there I would have them transported to the building site with a police escort. Most would come as four boxes and would result in a Cape Cod style home being constructed in one day.

We started construction in late 2003. I took the lead as far as construction being started and accomplished. I had hired a fellow volunteer firefighter with Tisbury Fire Department, Andy Dixon, as Project Manager, responsible for building the units, coordinating subs and more. He also committed to buying one of the units. He worked very hard over the next few years and I'm thankful to have had him managing the project. It was never easy, and it took a lot my management and leadership skills to overcome each obstacle as they came up.

By 2007, the project was complete, and I am happy to say we all made a lot of money, but well within what the 40B regulations stipulated. I had wound up taking on most of the burden to get it done, from project approval, to overseeing construction, to dealing with the town, to completing financial forms for the 40B and to dealing with the community where I was well known. As I look back upon it, I can honestly say that it was the most significant and difficult work-related challenge I was ever faced with and accomplished, which includes rescuing people in fires to helping take American Ski Company public.

There were times when I was on Main Street in Vineyard Haven and I could feel people looking at me with animosity. I respected their opinion, but at the end of the day, I know that what we built was needed and done well. The project was called "Fairwinds," but clearly the name didn't reflect the actual tornado that took place. I did learn that I could handle being scrutinized, even hated and talked about. It was good training for what it would take when I finally came out as trans in later years.

One of my last serious fires and the road sign that made me rethink my career. Six months later I was working at Killington Ski Resort in Vermont.

The firefighting team at the 1980 Winter Olympics in Lake Placid. I am in the blue turtleneck.

1980- One of the greatest sporting events of all times and I was there!

Tom picketing in front of Arlington Fire Headquarters in 1982.

Taking American Ski Company public in 1997 at the New York Stock Exchange

Teri and Tom at our 20-year vow renewal at Canyons Ski Resort in 2013.

Lorraine and me at Lourdes high school reunion in 2011

Living to my personal mission- Women's March Park City 2017

Cami at Diva Las Vegas in 2018

Teri and Tom in 2015 at a friend's wedding. One of the last Tom pictures as transitioning was right around the corner.

Chapter 20

In early summer 2008, Teri and I sat on our porch of the Vineyard house, looking down at Lake Tashmoo, sipping our nightly cocktails and had a major discussion about our future and where we would live. I told her, "We can't keep making these huge mortgage payments, especially on the Vineyard and Florida house." We weighed keeping the Vineyard house, but it didn't make sense as the mortgage was huge and although we loved the summers there, we didn't like being stuck on the island during the winters. Sarasota was a viable option, but again the mortgage was huge, and we didn't think we could live in Florida in the heat of the summer. I looked at refinancing and was told by the bank that we weren't in default and there was nothing they could do for us, basically implying stop making payments, so we decided to stop making payments on those two homes and see what develops.

The houses went on the market along with many other homes from people like us who were overleveraged. Although they were beautiful homes, they sat there unsold for almost 18 months. We kept lowering the price, but still nothing. Finally, the bank, which was Countrywide, who later would go bankrupt, started foreclosure proceedings on both and put them up for short sales. We were renting them whenever we could and did still go to them, but only for short vacations. We held our last big Vineyard blowout party in October 2009 for Teri's 50th birthday and it was a fond farewell. All our close friends and family came, and it was a night to remember, although bittersweet. We loved our Vineyard home, having built it ourselves and took great pride in it. It had beautiful gardens loaded with blue hydrangeas thanks to our ownership in our nursery/garden center.

These decisions left us with our best and only living option, which was our Utah house. We loved the summers there and being big skiers, the winters were more than welcomed.

We had bought the house in 2004 from the ranch boss at the Diamond J Ranch. Teri and I were running the ranch as the Hospitality managers in the winters when the B&B was quiet, for a friend who owned it. The ranch boss had built the home, but couldn't afford the mortgage, so he asked us if we would buy it, so that he could move into the ranch's guest house where we were staying for free. We loved the area, so (and in hindsight thank God) we bought it from him. At the time I thought, what's one more house. It was brand new and was the perfect ski getaway. It's a blessing we bought it.

We decided to move full time to Utah and would move our retail business Beadniks with us to a new location in Park City. In August 2008, we made the move permanently. Beadniks was moved and rebuilt in the Redstone Center and opened in September 2008. It was even more beautiful than the St. Armands store and we proudly opened the doors. Unfortunately, it was just as the Wall St. banks were failing. Talk about bad timing. It never really generated any profits and we wound up needing Teri to manage it, to keep expenses as low as possible. She ran it for us for 3 years before we closed it in 2011 when the lease came up. We never took home a dime from operating it and the only thing good from it was the losses we could claim on our taxes. Between both locations we lost all our investment of over $500k.

Money was tight, but we were surviving as we had sold the garden center in 2008 to the General Managers, which was a pre-arranged deal when they were hired. We wound up taking back a second mortgage on the business as they did an SBA loan and the bank wouldn't loan them the money unless we held a sizable second. I was pissed off that we didn't get all our money at closing as it was to be our profit. As it turns out, thank god we had that income stream going forward as they were diligent about paying on time and it kept us going at a time when we needed income.

It wasn't until May of 2010 that the Vineyard and Sarasota homes both sold under short sales at crazy low prices. Once closed we were driving into Park City on a beautiful spring evening with the top down in our shiny red Audi convertible. They both had sold within a week of each other. We were going out to celebrate them selling. Teri has always trusted me with our finances and was aware of what was going on but didn't know all the dirty details. She asked, "So how did this turn out financially for us?" She knew we were losing money; she just didn't know how much. I responded, "How much do you think we lost?" She said, "I don't know, $250k?" I laughed and said, "Not even close. Try $750k." She looked at me in disbelief and said, "And we're going out celebrating?" I said, "Well, the bleeding is over, and we can finally move on." It was truly amazing that we survived all of this as we really had gotten ourselves (and I take the blame as I was "addicted to the deal") in a financial mess.

Teri was always a rock and willing to do whatever it took to make these businesses work. She was totally involved in running the B&B, helped manage the garden center becoming quite knowledgeable on plants and how to grow them and then managed the retail bead store.

In 2011, after we closed Beadniks she wanted to find work and applied for an $11/hour job as a front desk person at the local health clinic in Park City. She didn't get hired! We were shocked and amazed, but about a month later she got a call to ask if she was still interested and since she hadn't found anything yet, she took the job. As I write this book in mid-2019, I am proud to say she is now the RN Clinical Manager at the new Intermountain Urgent Care/Work Med clinic managing the entire operation. She is simply amazing in so many ways. I couldn't have found a better business and life-long partner.

It was a crazy 11 year stretch of entrepreneurialism. As I look back on it and write about it, it sounds worse than it was living thru it.

Chapter 21

In April 2015, I turned on the news to hear that Bruce Jenner had come out as a transgender woman and would now be known as Caitlyn. She explained how she had been hiding her transgenderism since childhood. That struck home for me. It really made me think about myself and what I had been hiding for years as well. Was I transgender or just someone who cross-dressed often? If she could come out, as famous of a male athlete that she was, then I could certainly look into that reality.

Some 6 years earlier, in 2009, I had told Teri about my feminine desires. By telling her I took the biggest chance of my life knowing full well it could end our marriage. Her first reaction was confusion. "What do you mean you like to dress up as a woman?" It was hard to explain to her, but I told her that I had been dressing for years, including during our marriage. The more she heard the more she felt I was leading a secret life. I had to agree but told her that was why I was telling her. She asked about my sexuality. "Are you gay?" I then explained that gender identity and sexuality identity are different. I told her that I was still a heterosexual person and that I still desired a woman, that woman being her. It was hard to hear her say, "Well, I'm sad and sickened. I feel this presents a lot of uncertainty in our marriage. I'll need more time to digest all this." Although I felt an amazing sense of relieve that I had finally come clean and told her, I was nervous it could change our relationship dramatically and I knew there would be a lot more to discuss. I had to tell her as the burden of sneaking around was tearing me apart. I had to believe she would be accepting.

Day after day we talked about it and having time to think about it, she asked a lot of pertinent questions. I was as vulnerable as I have ever been. After a stressful week she said she understood. Being a Registered Nurse, she knew that this was a psychological issue and wasn't to be dismissed as a lark or a hobby. After a difficult period of time she said I could continue dressing, as long as it was under some controls, so that she still had a man in her life. This plan started out with me having to ask her permission to dress when she was around, and it would be limited to a few days a week. It sounded workable to me and since anything would be better than nothing, I quickly agreed. I asked her when I could dress up in front of her and we agreed on a date. I was so nervous as I got ready and put on my makeup. I wanted to look as feminine as I could. When I came down from our bedroom, I was a nervous as I have ever been. She looked at me closely and offered her critique. She didn't laugh, which was a positive. I could accept her criticisms and tried to incorporate them into my look. I had crossed a big threshold in our relationship and came out with an accepting, although hesitant spouse.

Months went by quickly and I was loving the freedom of not hiding any longer from her. I have always been one that if you give me an inch, I will take a foot, so it wasn't long before a few days per week became almost every day. Her acceptance was growing, and surprisingly she didn't get mad at me for overstepping the bounds we set. I was living two different lives, one as Tom and the other as Cami, which was difficult, but worth it as I loved the thrill of dressing as a woman. Dressing motivated me every day. I liked experimenting with looks and makeup. I was well aware it was both addicting and narcissistic and I spent way too much time looking at myself in the mirror. We would often go out for date night, but we would go to Salt Lake City where I wasn't as well-known, and we could be incognito.

After we talked about Caitlyn Jenner, she recommended that I see a therapist, who specializes in gender dysphoria. I had been putting it off for a long time and knew it was time to sort things out. I found a woman psychologist who specialized in dealing with the transgender community, named Deanna Rosen, out of Salt Lake City.

My first appointment was nerve-wracking as I had never confided in someone the way I would have to with her. She listened, and she counseled me. I finally opened up about my struggles with dressing after almost fifty years. I told her stories about my life that I had never shared and was afraid to even admit or face. After a few months of some very difficult "Come to Jesus" moments, she confirmed that I was transgender. I always sensed it, but now had confirmation. She said, "You're transgender, now what will you do?" I knew what I wanted to do. I wanted to go full time, but I had some obstacles to overcome. I was tired of constantly living two lives, hiding in my house and always fearful of being caught. It was no way to live and I had had enough. My fear of what others would think was slowly evaporating and my confidence to go full time was building. I knew a lot of trans women by this point in time and I would hear their stories and become jealous. I thought about what challenges I would face, but I knew it was what I had to do, wanted to do and would do.

I felt confident in telling a good friend from Park City, John Wells, in October 2015. He was the first person other than Teri that I would tell. He was incredibly accepting, and I knew I had a strong ally. In October 2015, I called my sister Terry and brother Jim and told them both. It was National Coming Out Day. As I expected, they were very accepting, but curious. I had crossed another major hurdle and was building confidence in what still had to happen.

Chapter 22

The time had come for me to take action, so in February 2016, I sat with Teri and nervously asked, "What do you think about me coming out as transgender and living full time as Cami?" It would be a huge decision for us to make and could be a make or break situation. It turns out it would be the most impactful thing I would ever do. We had some very candid conversations about what it would mean to our relationship now and long-term.

She had concerns, most important were her concerns over what people will think about us and our relationship. She asked, "How will they view me?" She maintains to this day that she is not interested in pursuing a lesbian relationship and still has difficulty in showing affection with me in public. I was dressing as Cami almost all the time at this point and would only be dressed as Tom while going to work at the Temple and if we were going out together in Park City. She was comfortable with that arrangement, but I was throwing a monkey wrench in the works. She knew I really wanted to take this big step and it was very considerate of her to even consider my request.

After lots of discussion she agreed and said, "Ok, lets tell everyone! You can be the person you want to be." I was ecstatic, but we both knew this would open her and me up to a lot of criticism and questions. In agreeing, she showed true courage and amazing commitment to me and our marriage.

The yearly Killington ski trip was coming up and I knew what I had to do, it was just a question as to if I had the "guts" to do it. I told Teri, "I am going to go back east and tell Erin and Lindsay and then everyone on the ski trip."

The girls were going to be difficult and I prayed they would understand and be accepting. I knew their personalities were to be accepting people, but I wasn't sure how they would react. I was very nervous as I boarded the plane from Salt Lake City to Boston. I knew I was facing one of the biggest challenges I would ever face. I prepared some thoughts of what to say and hoped I could remember them when it was time.

Erin picked me up from the airport in Boston. In the car on the way to her house and out of the clear blue I blurted out, "I need to tell you something about me that I have been hiding for a long time. I have been diagnosed as being transgender," which was nothing close to what I had prepared to say. She was shocked, and after she collected her thoughts, she asked some logical questions, which I tried to honestly answer.

"How long have you felt this way?"

"I can remember wearing my mother's clothes when I was 8 years old, so a long time. I've been fighting the realities of who I am for 55 years."

"Are you gay?"

"No, gender identity and sexual preferences are completely different. I am still hetero-sexual and interested in women, specifically Teri."

"Are you going to have surgery?

"No plans to do so at this point and I haven't really discussed it seriously with Teri."

"Speaking of Teri, are you going to stay with her?"

"If she will still have me, yes. Believe it or not, she has been very accepting of all this"

After a while she started to cry. It was not something she expected to hear. She was confused. I immediately knew it would take her awhile to grasp what it meant.

She said, "I'm sad that you had to wait so long to say anything." She was very concerned about Teri and how she was feeling about the news. In the days and weeks that followed I would have many subsequent conversations with her to help her understand. She has become very accepting and I am fortunate to have such an amazing daughter.

Lindsay would be next as we were driving to her house for dinner. Erin said she wouldn't say anything. We had a great dinner and after Erin left, I asked Lindsay to come with me to their playroom where I nervously told her, in a talk that was much closer to what I had prepared.

She heard me out fully, gave me a hug and said, "I love you no matter what. If this is what you want to do, I will support you." Whew, what a relieve. She asked many of the same questions Erin had asked and again, I answered them all. I felt relieved that I had told both my daughters and still felt loved.

I was nervous about her husband Michael as he tends to be somewhat conservative. After he realized we had been gone awhile, he yelled out, "Where are you guys" and Lindsay told him to come down to the playroom. I told him the news and after shocking him for sure, he gave me a bear hug and said, "No issues here. Do what you want to do." Although I was hoping they both would agree to allow telling my grandkids, who were 7 and 5 at the time, they wanted to wait awhile as they didn't think they would understand what it meant. Although I was disappointed, I reluctantly agreed that I needed to do so on their time schedule, not mine. I would eventually wait until the summer of 2017 until we told them.

The next day I would leave the girls and go on my annual Killington ski trip where it would be time to tell friends and some family. It would be a complete surprise to tell them that I was transitioning and would be presenting myself as a female 24/7 and that I would from then on be known as Cami.

Why Cami? Well, I chose Cami as a name for the stupidest of reasons. For many years while in hiding I was known as Cami Desiree. I decided on that name because it sounded sexy and I never thought it would wind up being a permanent part of me going forward. I dropped the name Desiree after a call from my close friend Brian when he told me that some of my friends were talking about me and suggested that I drop Desiree as It sounded sleazy. I couldn't agree more so I dropped it soon after when I closed my second Facebook page where I was known as Cami Desiree.

One of my best friends in life is Scott Karn. We have known each other for over 40 years. He and I drove up together to Vermont as we always had for seven prior years. In the car ride I was very nervous. I was as vulnerable as I have ever been and told him about me being trans. I could see in his face his initial confusion and concern. He listened intently and tried and take it in. I don't think he believed me. Initially, he seemed accepting, but in subsequent conversations he expressed his concerns. He asked about my relationship with Teri and how it was going to survive. He and Teri were very close, and he truly loved her and had deep concerns for her welfare. I did my best to answer his questions truthfully and was very vulnerable. It's hard to tell someone who has been one of my closest friends something so impactful.

Over time and after many deep conversations and him finally realizing that I am the same person, he and I are still the best of friends and like brothers from a different mother.

I remember being nervous as all hell when telling some other long-time friends, Steve and Martha Ellicott. They have been good friends for many years, and I wasn't sure how they would react. They were shocked and promised to take it all in and try to adjust to it. I think they are still working on full acceptance and our relationship is different than it once was, but I am still hopeful.

I told another great friend and my best man Brian Ganey. Brian can be very deep, yet thoughtful. He is very liberal and easily accepted what I had told him. He hugged me and I knew he was on board. He has remained one of my closest friends and I love him like a brother. We talk often and there isn't much he doesn't know about Cami.

Chapter 23

I had crossed one major hurdle in my coming out, but I still had my hometown friends in the Park City area to tell. For the time being, I would still dress as Tom while working at Temple Har Shalom, where I had been serving as Executive Director for a few years, but would-be Cami wherever else I went, even in Park City. We scheduled a dinner-party for about 30 of our closest Park City friends and it turned out that almost everyone attended. The date would-be March 29th, 2016. We sent out invitations about three weeks prior.

One night about a week before the party, I was out with my good trans girlfriend, Zoe Goode. We had met a year earlier and quickly became fast friends. We shared many of the same beliefs and our paths were similar. She was a successful architect in the Boston area and was married to a loving spouse who was trying to understand why their husband was coming out as trans. Our true connections were that she was a big skier, like me, with a 2nd home at the base of Snowbird/Alta and she loved live music and dancing. She was a natural fit.

We were out dancing at The Spur on Main Street in Park City where I would often go to as Cami. This is a great dance club/bar with local cover bands. It is loaded with locals, which always made for a fun evening mixed with tourists here to ski the world class resorts of Deer Valley and Park City Mountain. It had a great vibe, but most importantly I was welcomed with open arms. The owner became a friend. I was not a stranger to the dance floor when I noticed two friends walk in and out of the clear blue one of the guys, who had been invited to the party, came up to me, stared at me carefully and with a confused look asked, "Is that you Tom?"

I had been outed! I quickly responded by saying, "Yeah, it's me." In retrospect, I should have said, "It's a Halloween costume," but it was March, not October. I quickly added, "I should tell you now that the reason for the party Saturday night is for me to announce to all of you that I am coming out as transgender." He looked shocked and confused, so I continued to explain what it all meant. He was a little drunk, so after a while he seemed to take the news in good stride that night. My good friend, J W, who knew about me was with him and said to him on the way home, "Al, keep your mouth shut and don't tell anyone." Well, keeping secrets is not his nature. By the time the party came, it turns out that he told someone, who told someone else and at the end of the day, about seven of those attending knew in advance, which probably explains the high attendance. I am glad I found this out after the party as I am not sure how I would have reacted, but most likely with anger. This was such an unfair thing to have done to me. It is commonly understood in society that it was up to me to tell my friends, family and community and someone should never be outed to others without permission. I'm not sure if he ever really got the message that what he had done was completely wrong. He never really apologized properly, and we have subsequently been just acquaintances and our friendship has clearly been hampered.

Early in the evening I asked everyone at the party to please go into the family room. I sensed some people thought that I was going to tell them that Teri and I were splitting up. I. I was shaking like a rattlesnake and as sincere and humble as I have ever been. I stood in the doorway and read the following very heartfelt letter explaining what I had decided:

To end the drama, I am not dying, and Teri and I are fine and not divorcing. I need a big favor from all of you, which is to hold all your comments till the end of what I am about to say. Also, this is not a joke and not something to laugh at. It is very serious to me.

I must admit that I feel very nervous and humbled to tell you this, but here goes...

First off, all of you are dear friends who I care about and love very much.

A year ago, a significant news event occurred that caused me to look closely at something that I have been living with for many, many years.

I started seeing a therapist and after many sessions, I was diagnosed as being transgender, which is something that was not surprising to hear, as I believe I've had known this for a while but didn't want to admit it out of fear and embarrassment.

I have decided to accept this diagnosis and I am comfortable with it, which is why I am finally able to tell you. So, what does it mean to be transgender to me? Being transgender in essence means that the gender identity that I was born as, that being male, is no longer who I can identify with, but rather I identify better as a female.

I have lived with this for many years as it started in my childhood. Teri has known since 2009 and has been both accepting and loving. She has been simply amazing and is my true soul mate. I have kept this inside of me for many years and it is an amazing relief to finally tell all of you. I can now end the deceit, hiding and lies with all my friends and family, who I told last month.

Since I don't want this to be a burden on you, the logical question is what's in it for you? If you get anything out of this it will hopefully be that you are better accepting and educated about the LGBT community, as now even one of your friends is part of it. Also, and this is only a good feeling kinda thing, you should know that I think so highly of all of you that I would have the courage to bare my soul to you.

This may surprise some of you and maybe some of you are saying, "I knew it." I think there have been some obvious telltales in my male appearance, (nails, being shaved, tight jeans and the occasional makeup) to which not once have any of you ever made a derogatory comment, which I truly have appreciated. So, what will this mean to you? Probably very little, if anything, as I still will be Tom for the foreseeable future and continue to live this double life. However, I do promise if I play from the women's tees, you will get more strokes if needed.

I am not just jumping on the transgender bandwagon because it's in the news a lot. It is just time for me to be real with myself. By the way, that big event that occurred a year ago was Caitlyn Jenner coming out, who had a lot of influence on me when she did that and I thought if she could do it, so could I. I will also say that thanks to her, public acceptance and genuine interest in the trans community is remarkably different.

I have met many great friends in the trans community and participate as much as I can in support of the LGBTQ+ community, in fact, I am going to Vegas next week as I am one of the organizers of one of the largest transgender outings in the country with over 150 people from all over the US and even Europe attending. I am very proud to call myself a trans woman.

To end any speculation, I have no plans of transitioning at this time, as Teri is the most important person in my life and at this time, this is her preference. Also, I am still heterosexual, which may confuse some of you, but let me simply say that trans people fall into a wide spectrum of sexual preferences that are all over the place. There is no right or wrong, just who one is, whether it be straight, bisexual, gay or whatever.

I promise you that I will never intentionally put you in a difficult position without warning or asking you in advance. Although, you may be out sometime and see me as Cami, which is my alter ego name, so if you do, act as you must.

Teri and I have typically gone out in SLC but in the future Park City is going to be a place where we want to go out and feel comfortable doing so. If confronted by a friend, we will deal with those that are just discovering Cami for the first time. I have the strength to do so now.

I would really appreciate you keeping this amongst all of us here. Please refrain from spreading the word around town as I still am at the Temple and I want to keep them out of the loop as long as possible. Although if it gets out, so be it.

So, I am on this crazy journey and not sure where it will take me and Teri, but I now believe I have the opportunity for acceptance, love, friendship and have the strength I need to be comfortable going forward. Let me leave you with this thought: There is an old saying that goes "The more things change the more things stay the same." As it relates to what I just told you, what that means is "I may look different in the future, but it is what is inside of me that matters and that will not change".

At the end and with me in tears, she and I were warmly approached by every single person who offered their support and love. Some would change their position later; some would want to find out more and some acted if there was nothing ever different in our relationship. It was interesting to hear some of the women remark, "I knew something was different with you." This was an obvious reference to me always having polished, clear nails, body shaved all over, light makeup and dying my hair. One might say I was vain and narcissistic, and I would have to agree.

Later on, at that coming out, I explained the difference between sexual identity and gender identity by saying, "The best way to think about it is that sexual orientation is who you go to bed with, indicating that you might be gay, lesbian, bisexual or heterosexual. Gender identity is who you go to bed as, which can be a male, a female and whatever way the trans person presents themselves." Think of gender as how the person feels on the inside. I had told tell them that I am still a heterosexual person in the traditional sense, meaning I like women, that being my wife Teri, but I present myself as a transwoman. I think most people get confused and think that since I present myself as a female, I am interested in men. Well, I am not interested in men, just women, some like to call this being a Trans lesbian. There are many trans people who are interested in men. It can be confusing, and people can often stereotype the situation. Simply put, sex and gender are all over the map. There is no one answer.

On the same note, the things I wish I had told them about is what is okay to ask a trans person or better said, what isn't okay to ask, which is, "Do you still have all your normal parts, or did you have the operation, or in other words, "Do I still have a penis?" Another one is, "Do you sleep with men?"

There are others. "How do you and how often do you have sex? When did you become transgender? Are you a transvestite? (Which is insulting to some.) What bathroom do you use? Will you go back to your old self?"

If the trans person wants to share this type of information with you, it is okay for you to keep the conversation going until they want to end it. It is best to walk a careful line until a level of comfort exists between you both.

One thing I would encourage is for you to be open and welcoming to trans people and it is okay for you to approach us. Often friends say to me that they see that I am so welcomed out in public. People come up to me often and just say "Hi."

At times, I see things differently. Most people just walk by, but if we make eye contact (or not) I can immediately see on some face's judgment and/or confusion. Some shake their head in disgust or make a passing comment. I see it and hear it. I don't get upset. Instead, I see that the trans community still has a long way to go to change perceptions of us. I get energized and my spirit grows stronger.

Chapter 24

The day after the announcement party, one of my good friends named Frank Dwyer called me. It was a Sunday and he said that he wanted to meet me for lunch at a bar/restaurant that he owns on Monday. He said he had been on the internet all-day reading up more about transgenderism and had some questions. So, the next day we met for lunch at The Boneyard, a local's favorite in Park City. I was excited that he took the time to find out more information and then to want to meet with me to ask me about it. We had a long enlightening conversation, but it would still take him awhile to understand it and to come to grips that his one-time male friend Tom, would now be presenting himself as a female. What's been interesting to see develop is that some of my long-time friends, who knew Tom, have a much harder time accepting me now then people who have met me only as Cami for the first time. They never knew Tom and have accepted me for who I now am and choose to be.

The summer of 2016 proceeded along with me being out and about as Cami at concerts, shopping and ultimately into the golf community playing as Cami. At the beginning of the season I was playing as Tom and was openly excepted by my fellow golf friends. I started to notice a change as the season went on as Cami and I found myself being cut-out of a foursome that I used to play with regularly. I just had to accept the fact that it was going to take some time for most of those guys to except me presenting myself as a female.

One evening at a Deer Valley concert, I had an amazing encounter with a total stranger. I was sitting on my blanket listening to the music when this woman came and sat directly in front of me looked at me and said, "My name is Phyliss, I am conservative, a Christian, and a Republican and I've been told that I should hate people like you. Please tell me why I shouldn't?"

At that very minute, I was struck with confusion as to how to respond but I launched into my personal story, so that she could have a better understanding of me and what I was all about. We had an amazing conversation and after about twenty minutes she left my blanket, gave me a big hug and a kiss and said "Thank you. I get it now." In fact, she wanted to know when she could see me again as she was in town for a few days doing work for her company from Texas. She wound up showing up the following night at a different concert in Kimball Junction and sat with me and my wife. By the end of our two day encounter I think I had converted her to be a person who can be much more loving and accepting of the LGBTQ community. There are very bright moments, and this was one of them.

In July, just before I went on vacation back to Martha's Vineyard, I was sitting at a local Park City bar called the Boneyard on the sun deck upstairs. It is absolutely spectacular with great views of Deer Valley and Park City Mountain. I had been going there often that summer as Cami, and the staff was very accepting of me.

I wound up sitting alongside two people, who both are KPCW radio hosts on a show called "The Mountain Life." They weren't supposed to know who I was, but the woman, Lynn, quickly looked at me and said without hesitation, "Hi Cami." I was startled! She said she had been told about me by my good friend J W, who was the first friend I shared my Cami identity with. She was very welcoming. With her was her radio co-host Tim Henning, who also warmly greeted me.

We had a wonderful conversation and it wound up with them asking me to come on their show and be interviewed about what it is like being transgender in Park City. I was thrilled. On the morning of the interview I showed up at KPCW radio excited but apprehensive. We had discussed the fact that I would still have to remain only identified as Cami and not as Tom, as people at the Temple were not yet aware of me coming out as trans. The interview went exceptionally well. The more I spoke the more confident I was. The more questions they asked, the more I felt that I was getting my message out. They quickly asked, "What it was like to be transgender in Park City?" This was easy to answer. "Park City is the most liberal and accepting community in Utah, a bit of a bubble. 1ql hear their curiosity, but I am very supported," I replied.

The questions were all over the spectrum. "Is a trans person homosexual? What is the difference between transsexual and transgender? Were you hardwired to be a female? Was your previous life a charade? Trans marriages don't survive, why does yours? What is your sexual preference? What was it like telling your daughters? What is it like to be on the street as a man dressed as a woman? Are you trapped in the wrong body? Is it possible for the radio audience to relate to being trans? Will I undergo surgery? Are you on hormones? Why does gender matter?" Some were easy and some were hard to answer, but I did my best and answered each question as honestly as possible.

I recall some significant comments I made. "I am on a journey and not sure where it will go." "I promised my friends that I would never place them in an uncomfortable position." "I want to be an ambassador and educator to the trans community." I left feeling I had a great interview and that those listening got something out of it. I would soon find out that I would get even more out of it.

It turns out that the President of the Temple, Ruth Davidson, had been listening to the interview on the radio and was putting two and two together. Once I was finished, she called me and asked me if I wanted to come out to the Temple as transgender, which would allow me to present myself as a female full-time and live my life as a female 24/7. It was a welcome opportunity, but I still wasn't sure. I needed a push and it would quickly come.

The day after the radio interview, I was also contacted by the editor of the *Park Record,* the local newspaper, who said that she would like to run a story about me. There was one big hitch, which was that she wanted me to disclose my full name, Tom Richardson, which I hadn't done in the radio interview. I saw this as an opportunity to finalize my coming out, but there were some obstacles in the way, including the fact that Teri had not told anyone at her place of work. I spoke with Teri and she said she would tell the staff at her workplace, which was an urgent care clinic in Park City. I then told Ruth that I wanted to take her up on her offer and to come out at the Temple. It didn't take me long to agree to do the newspaper interview as well.

One powerful Temple board member, Barry Baker, was someone that I needed to tell. After Ruth and I discussed that we would make the announcement to the whole Board at the September board meeting, I went up to visit Barry, which happened to be five days before the August board meeting. I sat in his spacious office overlooking all of Park City somewhat nervous.

Following some other discussion, I just came out and said, "Barry, I have decided to come out as transgender full time and would like your approval to do so at the Temple." At first, he was confused and said he needed to understand more of what that meant. I think I surprised the hell out of him. Once we discussed it more, he looked at me and said, "Temple Har Shalom is a place of acceptance. We will have no problem allowing you to transition." I was overwhelmed with anticipation of what was to come and on the way home I was ecstatic. I couldn't believe my dream would be coming true.

I left that meeting knowing that I would soon be able to tell everyone at the Temple. The same afternoon I got a phone call from Ruth, who said that the Executive committee had met by phone and that she saw no reason to not bring this up at the August board meeting. Barry had intervened and pulled off his magic. So, 5 days later at the board meeting, I was warmly accepted by the Board and it was decided that that next day I could come out as Cami to the Temple.

I was excited beyond belief when I showed up to work on August 11th as Cami at the Temple. I've learned a lot about the Jewish faith in my tenure at the Temple and one thing that I clearly discovered is how open and accepting reformed Jews can be. There was no backlash at all despite my concerns that some members might be offended and leave their membership. My staff was just wonderful and fully accepting. It took a while to use the right name and pronouns, but they were willing to keep working at it. They were great and I love them all.

Right after, this newspaper story would come out, which would mean that I could now live my life 24/7 as Cami. It read as follows:

Transgender resident says community has been supportive

Park City | August 26, 2016

Nan Chalet Noaker

The Park Record

Known to many Parkites as Tom Richardson, Cami Desiree has come out as transgender. She said the overall reaction has been positive and supportive. ☐Nan Chalat Noaker/Park Record

Lots of people are apprehensive about attending their high school reunions. Memories of teenage angst and self-doubt can resurface, even decades later. But for Cami Desiree, who will attend her 45th high school reunion next month, the event is especially complex. The last time she saw her classmates, she was Tom Richardson.

But, she says, closing the gap between her past and present lives is also liberating.

At age 63, Cami says she is happy with the way her life has turned out, although she has some regrets about not coming out as transgender sooner. It has been a long journey, but many friends and acquaintances from all across the country are just now learning that the woman greeting them with a familiar smile is the person they used to know as a man.

Looking back, she realizes there were indications her gender identity didn't fit into the traditional mold beginning when she was eight years old and delighted in wearing her mom's clothes.

"I always knew that there was something different about me. I always felt it was something I couldn't share. I was raised in a very Catholic family … just the thought of this being found out was scary," she said.

And she did not fully shed that fear of being "found out" until earlier this month when she left Tom's wardrobe at home in the closet and went to work dressed as Cami.

Until then — first as a firefighter in New York, then CFO for American Skiing Company, later as a local entrepreneur and, currently, executive director of Temple Har Shalom – she was Tom. Cami was a closely held secret even from her spouse and children.

"It was hidden, very discreet. I had two kids. Life was just moving along. But it was something I knew was still there. It made me feel good when I was dressed as a woman. It made me feel like I was who I wanted to be," she said.

Five years ago, as LGBT communities across the country accelerated their fight for equality, Cami says she made a personal commitment to reconcile her two identities.

"In 2010, I decided I had to get real. I realized my wife is an amazing woman who deserves to know the truth and I had to take the risk she would potentially say 'it's not for me.' And it wasn't like it was a cakewalk, we had some serious discussions about what it all means, what was I doing."

Cami said she is lucky. "She is an amazing and loving spouse and I feel very fortunate to have her in my life."

They are still married and working through the transition together, Cami said.

Cami also made the difficult decision to share the news with her two adult children.

"My kids were great. My son-in-law is somewhat conservative, and they have two kids so I thought if this doesn't go well, he could say 'you can't ever see the kids again.' That's what held me back for a while. Instead they said, 'why did you wait so long?'"

At about the same time, Cami and her spouse, who had homes in Martha's Vineyard, Massachusetts and Sarasota, Florida, decided to move to Utah full time. They bought a home in Kamas and worked in Park City. Tom became well known in the community through his Park City Locals Card and Summit County Beef and together, the couple also ran two small local businesses.

Then, in 2015 when Bruce Jenner, the Olympic decathlete, made his public transition to Caitlyn, Tom decided to introduce Cami to his close friends. In March, she and her spouse threw a party.

The response, she said was heartwarming.

Their friend Rob Schumacher was one of the guests and he remembers, "It didn't bother any of us. We were somewhat surprised, but we thought, 'That's just who he is.'" As far as Schumacher is concerned, "Tom/Cami, it's the same person. It doesn't feel awkward. We play golf, we have a good time."

Their friend John J.W. Wells who knew Cami as Tom for eight years before she transitioned, agrees. According to Wells, Cami confided in him about a year ago.

"There were some concerns that some friends would not be as accepting, but that's natural," Wells said adding, most people in Park City don't care if Cami wears a dress or men's pants. "Either way, he is just a dear friend," said Wells.

But it was still months before 'Tom' went to the office as 'Cami.' The transition announcement was carefully coordinated at the temple. In order to give congregants ample time to adjust, the news was first posted in the e-newsletter on Aug. 11. The next day she arrived at work as Cami.

Since then she has embraced her transgender identity full time.

"The simple answer is that it has gone very well. A number of people have reached out to me. They have been amazingly receptive," she said.

"Park City is a bubble. If you are looking for the best place to come out and be transgender, this is pretty good," she said.

During a recent outdoor concert at Deer Valley, Cami recounts how a stranger sat down on her blanket, leaned forward and confessed: "I am a Republican. I am from Texas. I am conservative. I'm Christian and I've been told I need to hate you." They ended up talking and parted with a hug.

Cami says the experience has also been positive outside of Park City. This week, while she was walking her dog along a side street in Kamas, a neighbor pulled up beside her and said, "I just want to tell you how brave I think you are."

As to that reunion with her classmates in Poughkeepsie, New York, Cami says some of the stress has been reduced. One of the organizers took it upon herself to email *attendees a gentle explanation that their former classmate Tom is now Cami and she hoped they would welcome her warmly.*

After her experience in Park City, Cami is confident that most will.

The newspaper article came out on August 26, 2016. It showed an old picture of me as Tom and one now of me as Cami. The longtime editor of the Park Record was Nan Chalat-Noaker and I thought she wrote an excellent recap of my story and coming out as trans. The entire community was exposed to what in many cases was the first time anyone in Park City came out in this public a forum. It was time for me to now be me. Many in the Park City community read the story and left comments, all of which were uplifting. "You, Dear Cami, are a true Warrior!" "I admire your courage in following your heart." "I'm with you all the way and proud of you for taking this courageous step. Love you." "I always knew you were pretty special, but this is truly special." "Your strength is inspiring!!" "You are amazing." "Hugs. Such courage, grace and inspiration." "Love you both and to me you are one." My sister wrote, "Somehow I laugh when I think of you wearing Mom's clothes." I felt the love and was feeling confident.

Despite these great comments, I learned quickly that this journey that I just started would be one of the most difficult things I've ever had to do. In the years that have passed since I came out, I've seen a mix of reactions and some rejection. I've had both family and close friends ultimately say they really, "Don't want to get to know Cami." Hearing those words really hurt. I certainly realize that their would-be some backlash, but I certainly didn't expect to have some very dear friends throw me down the toilet, but some did. Teri always likes to tell me, "It's their loss, not yours." How true!

This can be really upsetting and discouraging, but in speaking with others and getting counsel from my amazing wife, I have learned that acceptance for some will take longer than others. Some need to first mourn the fact that their friend or family member has transitioned to be a female. I've learned a lot about myself and about other people in this transition. I think it comes down to the basics of how you want to live your life, and I choose Love, not Hate!

As for me, I want to live with an open mind to everyone. I have always been the type of person who maintains a friendship by staying in contact with the other person. I've come to realize that to some degree I may have been chasing friends versus truly be deserving of their friendship. I've discovered that you can't buy friendship. There must be mutual respect and commitment. I've also noticed that some of my older friends, those over 60, who have never experienced meeting a transgender person, have had the biggest difficulty in accepting me for who I am now. Some say that they need more time and that they need to get used to it. Some never gave it the time needed and have decided to end our friendship.

One in particular was truly disappointing. Teri and I had developed a very close relationship with a wonderful couple from Boston, Ma. when I first started at Sunday River Ski Resort in 1993. Over the years we visited each other at our homes and spent many ski vacations together in New England. Park City and at Vail, Colorado, where they owned a beautiful condo timeshare. In early 2016, we visited with them at Vail where I nervously told them I was transgender. I wasn't presenting myself as Cami, so I don't think they could fully grasp what I had told them, but they would quickly find out I was serious.

After telling them, we were enjoying cocktails in the owner's lounge when some friends of theirs joined us. Out of the clear blue, the female in the couple says, "I was in a lady's room recently and noticed someone standing with their shoe toes facing the wall while peeing. If trannies are going to use the lady's room, they should be sitting instead of standing." I was aghast that the subject even came up, but replied without hesitation, "Well, funny you mention that as I'm transgender and I would have to say that the person was in the wrong, as we all are aware of the unwritten rules and pure logic. I always sit down as does most everyone I know who identifies as trans. By the way, the word trannies is hurtful, we prefer transgender or just trans."

I was surprised that I said anything as I was still in the process of going 24/7 and my confidence was still developing. I looked at my friends for their reaction and it was obvious I took everyone by surprise. The cocktail party ended, and nothing was said about it amongst us and while we visited with them, they seemed fine and accepting. After a month of waiting for a response to an email, I wrote them again and in an email that finally followed I was told, "We do not want to meet Cami." I took that as an end to a 23-year relationship. I was really saddened. They were the first couple to reject me as their friend and it really hurt. The worst part was that Teri was a great friend of theirs as well and in the process, they cut her out as a friend as well. We talked about it but there was nothing we could do about it. I wrote them a note in response that was cordial and expressed understanding. Unfortunately, we have never heard from them again.

Obviously, I believe that I still am the same person and that despite my appearance if they were to give me a chance, they would find that I am the same person and that if they loved or liked me before they should still be able to do so.

Chapter 25

My golf career highlight was in 2016 and started the day I was to come out as Cami 24/7. The newspaper article about me transitioning was to come out on that Saturday in August and I was committing to being Cami fulltime from that day forward. It also happened to be the first day of the Men's Park City Golf Club Championship. I always have played in this tournament and wanted to this year as well but was concerned about how the men in the Men's League would react. I spoke to the pro about what was going down. After a minute of me explaining he looked at me and, "You want me to cover your back?" I said, "Yea, I do." He then said, "Well, plan on playing on Saturday." I awoke that day and my nerves and excitement levels were high. The article was a big deal as my secret would now be public in the Park City community. I imagined local friends reading this article over a coffee and being completely shocked and probably laughing and saying the unimaginable.

I dressed in my best ladies' golf clothes and headed out to the course. Since I play golf barefoot the golf outfit would only add to people's confusion. I had butterflies in my stomach when I was parking as I would be seen as Cami for the first time by my fellow golfers.

The golf match started poorly. On the first hole I was so nervous that I pulled my drive into a thicket of pine trees. It got uglier fast and I wound up taking an eight on the par 4 first hole of a two-day stroke play tournament, where every stroke count. I was 4 over par after one hole and felt I probably just played myself out of the tournament, which I normally do well in. I settled my nerves and played very well the rest of the round and wound up only 3 strokes back of the leader after round one. The next morning, I again woke up nervous, but not because of being Cami, but because I really wanted to win. It was a hot summer day, which works to my advantage normally. I was playing with and against the leader, so I would always know where I stood in the match. He bogeyed the first hole and I started off with a birdie. I was only one back right out of the gate. He didn't play well, and I could see he was nervous. I rose to the occasion and played well in the second round and won the division. I was thrilled. I have a great picture of me as Cami pointing to the final leaderboard of the Men's Club Championship where my name, which had been written as Tom on the board, but was later crossed out to be Cami, with the 1st place notation. I was so happy and proud, although I'm not sure many others who played felt the same way. I heard someone call me the 'Barefoot Contessa', which was somewhat true, so it became my new nickname.

Chapter 26

In September of 2016 I was invited to attend the 45th reunion of the Our Lady of Lourdes High School Class of 1971. It also happened to be a weekend that my former Arlington firefighters' union #2393 was having a golf tournament/fundraiser. I thought it would be a fantastic opportunity to go back and see former classmates, co-workers and friends and to have everyone meet Cami firsthand. I was rather nervous as I would also be seeing my brothers and sister at a family barbeque for the first time. I felt I just needed to be confident and it would all work out.

I sat next to a wonderful woman on my plane trip back east, whom I truly believe was sent to help me combat my fears, as our conversation was profound for me and her. She told me that she recently learned that her 18-year-old son was transgender and transitioning to be a female. It was one and a half hours into the flight before she mentioned it, after she asked me many pointed questions about being trans. "When did I know? How hard has it been? Do I have regrets?" Finally, she told me the truth and we spent the remaining flight hours talking about being transgender. I believe I really helped her understand more and at the same time, helped me answer some tough questions about myself. It was karma that we met. The trip was starting off well.

I woke up bright and early on Friday morning to get ready for the golf tournament. I had tried to touch base with an old shift mate of mine, whose name was Fish, short for Rich Fishwick. He and I go way back and have seen and done it all relative to partying, EMT and firefighting. We had been good friends and shift mates for many years. I reached out to him before I went and didn't hear back from him in the week before, but I finally heard from his wife the day before. She said he felt a bit apprehensive about meeting Cami but thought perhaps when he sees me it would change.

I showed up at the parking lot nervous as hell knowing that a bunch of rough and tough New York firefighters were going to be judging me. Ironically, I parked my car and was getting my clubs out when alongside me Fish pulled up in his truck. He got out, looked at me and I looked at him and I immediately knew that we still had our connection. After a rough first moment, it went fine. I played the day as Cami and got a chance to see a lot of other good friends from the old days. Although I'm sure they were saying things behind my back-and maybe even cracking a joke or laughing at me, I felt that I did something bold and that took courage.

I played on my brother's team. I must admit they were the biggest bunch of cheaters I have ever seen or played golf with. Their logic was, "Well the other teams are cheating, so to be competitive we have to as well." However, we still lost badly. It's funny, I have always been a very competitive golfer and the thought of cheating never crosses my mind. It's pretty amazing that my focus shifted from worry over how I'd be received to annoyance at the cheating!

Friday night was Alumni Homecoming night at a Friday night Lourdes football game. I was nervous as I slowly walked up to where we would all be eating some pre-game dinner. I was greeted by everyone and very warmly. After the game, we all went to a local bar that we used to go to and had a chance to meet and talk with old friends again. It was a wonderful evening and I did not feel slighted by anyone.

The next day was the night of the actual reunion dinner which was to be held at the Italian center in Poughkeepsie New York. Earlier that day, a bunch of us met and walked across the Hudson River on the walking trail, which is absolutely beautiful. I can vividly remember when it was a railroad trestle bridge and caught fire in early 1970's. It was one scary fire to fight.

I certainly spent a lot of time getting ready and making sure I looked my best. I was confident when I went into the reception area and once again was greeted warmly by all those that were there. Although I wasn't supposed to be the master of ceremonies the individual who was to be was a good friend and asked if I wanted to help him open up the evening. Of course, I said sure, as I am never one to shy away from a microphone. We both went up there and Tim started the evening by saying "Good evening and welcome. My name is Donna Joe Tortorella," who was the female head organizer, and everyone laughed. It was obviously a lead in for me.

He handed the microphone to me and dressed as Cami I said in a very inquisitive voice, "And my name is Tom Richardson?" Everyone laughed. It broke the ice and it worked out well.

The evening and celebration were just wonderful, and everybody treated me with respect and with plenty of questions and well wishes. I must admit that I looked very feminine and I think most attendees would agree that I looked pretty good for a guy dressed as a woman. At the end of the evening the woman who oversaw the event got up and spoke and said, "Our next anniversary will be our 50th and for that we need to do something big, maybe even have it on a cruise ship." But then she said, "And ladies, we can't let Cami look the best-of us all, so we got some work to do." I was humbled by her kind words, but I also felt bad for the other women in attendance who might have taken that as an insult, but no ill will was intended.

I awoke Sunday morning knowing that I would finally get to see my brothers John and Jim and sister Terry and their spouses at the barbecue. I hadn't seen any of them except for my sister whom I was staying with over the weekend. It was a beautiful day and I felt lots of love and respect. I think all people who are or have transitioned have a fear of being seen by friends and family for the first time and not feeling welcomed. This was hardly the case as I never felt threatened or scared somebody might say anything that would hurt my feelings.

When I came out to my older brother John and told him that I was trans earlier in 2016, I think it completely floored him. I believe he only remembers me as his tough brother, the good firefighter and someone he could depend on. I was his fellow Alabama football fan. This news was hard for him to accept. He never came out with any words of encouragement or verbal acceptance of me.

I would know how he truly felt soon enough. His stepdaughter Beth was getting married on New Year's Eve of 2016 and of course, Teri and I were invited. We quickly made our room and plane reservations. I was thrilled to think I would be going as Cami and be out to the entire family at a family function. My excitement became my worst nightmare when John texted me and said he didn't want me to go as Cami because, "I might steal the limelight from the bride. Come as Tom or don't come." I was being rejected by a close family member. Although I believe the bride might have felt differently, I'll never know for sure. She had to fall in line with what John and her mother felt. I wasn't about to cave into this pressure from someone who most likely did not like the idea of me coming out as trans to begin with, so Teri and I cancelled our plans to attend. I was devastated. I searched and hoped for a different answer but there was none to be found. Once again, I had to step back and realize that me transitioning isn't for everyone and some friends or family will take longer than others to accept.

The brother and the close connection we once had may be hard to repair, but I will keep trying. In our younger years, politics wasn't really discussed, but as we got older it was obvious that he became a very conservative Republican. I am a flaming liberal Democrat. It's amazing how we see things so completely differently. I don't see him, nor I, changing our beliefs and have resigned myself to a much different relationship.

Overall, it was a great weekend and one that I will never forget. I had broken the ice with almost all my family and friends at this point, but still had Teri's family to deal with Like Chappaquiddick there was a bridge to cross and it would prove to be difficult. What?

Chapter 27

So, at this point I was out fully to the Park City community, but not to all my friends. I decided that I would share the news on Facebook and prepared a post indicating what I had done and why, similar to the letter I read at my house party. I am sure this post surprised many of my long-time friends, but for the most part everyone responded with acceptance and encouragement. At least they did so at first and on social media.

I wrote the following on Facebook:

Dear Family and Friends,

Please take the time to fully read this as it is something important about me.

With all the vulnerability I can muster up, I want to tell all of you that I have proudly come out as being Transgender. After 63 years of hiding and keeping this a secret, I feel very liberated to come out to all of you, in fact I am thrilled and feel a big burden has now been lifted off my shoulders.

Let me try to explain a few things about being transgender. What it means is that I identify as a female and in the future, I will be presenting myself and living as a woman. My female name is Cami Desiree. Let me further explain that Gender identity, (i.e. if one identifies as male, female or trans) and Sexual identity, (i.e. If one identifies as being heterosexual, bisexual, gay or lesbian) are two different things. One can be trans and still be heterosexual.

I didn't just jump on the transgender bandwagon because it's the "in" thing. In fact, it's a very politically charged issue that many would run away from. But that's not my style. In fact, I have been an active member of the trans community for over six years and help organize one of the largest trans outings in the country in Vegas each spring. I realize that this may come as a shock to many of you. All I can say is that "it is what it is". I think you will find that if you meet Cami that I am the same person, just presenting myself as a female. For a long time, I would end any texts or emails with the phrase YOLO. It means "you only live once." Well, I feel pretty fortunate that I have lived an amazing life as Tom and now I get to live the rest of my life as Cami.

About seven years ago I came out to Teri Cook and she has been an amazing spouse in this journey, that we are both on. She has been a great counsel to me and showed me what true love, acceptance and compassion is all about. I am so fortunate to have her in my life.

Please feel free to friend me on my Cami Desiree page on FB. I will continue to use my Tom Richardson page but will likely tag Cami in most posts. If this is troublesome to you in any way or you would like to learn more, please feel free to message me directly. If you feel you don't want to follow me any longer, I will completely understand.

So, I hope you will bid Tom a fond farewell (in appearance only) and welcome Cami into your life.

Love, Cami

There was only one major hurdle left which was to tell her family. Teri's parents were still alive, and she also has twin brothers, who are one year younger. It's amazing the looks and similarities they share. They have both been married to wonderful women and have five children between them. Both live on the east coast and over the years we would spend time on vacation together, typically with them coming to our place on Martha's Vineyard. We were fairly close with them and I considered them family. We shared the same interests, such as golf, cooking, food, beaching and family.

Teri and I did not immediately tell them and waited till October. We also discussed how we would tell her brothers and who would tell them. We debated this repeatedly and finally decided that Teri would tell them, and I would be available for questions. In October of 2016, she made the phone call that would change many relationships dramatically. She told them, "Tom has come out as being transgender and is living full time as a female named Cami."

At first, they both appeared to take the news in stride, with the usual line, "People should live their life as they chose," but a few days after, Teri got a phone call from her brother John. The twins had spoken with each other and their spouses.

He said to her, "We have some problems with all this. We aren't happy that Tom didn't communicate with us directly. We feel that Tom deceived you and that your marriage has been a sham for all these years."

He went on further and said, "We insist that you tell Mom and Dad as they should know. They will find out from social media if you don't tell them and we don't want to be complicit in hiding this from them."

There wasn't much Teri could say to change their opinions and hung up knowing it was getting ugly fast.

She told me, and my reaction was, "Wow! That certainly didn't go as expected."

Her brothers' attitudes hurt and were confusing to me. They were entitled to their opinions, but why did it matter to them as long as Teri was accepting of me? There was also way more to the story that they didn't know about. I also question that if I had told them instead of Teri if their response would have been, "Why isn't Teri telling us this?" Either way, I couldn't win.

I reached out to their spouses to try to diffuse the situation. They appeared to be coming around a little and they suggested that I reach out to both brothers. I spoke to her brother Micky and after answering some questions and doing some explaining he eventually started to come around and said, "You are always welcome in our home." Unfortunately, I haven't heard a word from him since and I haven't been back to New York to visit to test the waters. Her other brother John responded via text and said, "When I am ready, I will reach out." He still hasn't and it's been years.

As for her parents, Teri and I had originally discussed whether to even tell her parents or not. Our original logic was simple, they were old and in ill health and what they didn't know, wouldn't hurt them. More importantly, her father could be someone who had traits of bigotry and racism in his personality. I started to see it more as he aged. I usually stayed away from issues that I knew would irritate him and it kept our relationship healthy.

We both agreed that telling him would likely result in me being excommunicated from the family. Upon hearing her brother's wishes, Teri was a dutiful sister and daughter and flew to Florida to tell them in November 2016. They had retired there about 25 years prior and lived in a 55 and older retirement community in Sun City Center developed by Dell Webb.

They both wondered why she would come visit them unexpectedly. After settling in and when the time was right, she told them. "Tom has come out as transgender and will be living full time as a woman from here out. She goes by the name Cami. Believe it or not, I am OK with all this and I accept her." They listened to what she said, and her father responded, "There is no way I can accept this." He further said, "As far as we are concerned, he is history to us." Unfortunately, that has been the case ever since.

She called me and told me the story and although I was crushed, I knew it was coming. They were older, Republican and conservative. They just didn't understand how anyone could be transgender, probably because they just never understood what it meant or had met someone transgender. I had been a loving son-in-law for almost 25 years, but that wouldn't matter. I believe they always loved me as well. I was heartbroken.

I had no contact with them from that date and through most of 2017. Teri and I knew there was a looming reality that would eventually happen. Both parents were old at 78 and 84 and we knew their passing would happen sooner than later. Her mother had cheated death in May 2017 after a golf cart accident. In October 2017, her father became very sick requiring hospitalization. The prognosis wasn't good, and he would require dialysis to stay alive.

I was fearing the day that either of them passes away as I knew I would not be welcomed at the services. I would be heartbroken to not be there to support Teri in her grief and to deal with my own grief of losing family I truly loved.

I flew down to Siesta Key in Florida to meet Teri on a prescheduled vacation in early November 2017. This had become our go-to place as it was close to her parents and was often voted the number one beach in America with its white talcum powder sand. We just love it there.

Teri had flown down a full week earlier to be with her father, who was in the hospital. He was in serious condition and she spent some quality time with him. It was difficult for me to know that his time was perhaps getting near and I couldn't see him.

The second day there, Teri got a phone call from her mother. I could immediately see in Teri's face that dreaded look. She looked at me and said, "Dad just died." The reality hit quick. Her father had just passed away, so Teri said, "I need to be with my mother. She is crying and parked in a Home Depot parking lot and not sure what to do." She told her mother to call their good friend Ray and ask for his help till she could get there.

Teri would need a ride to her Mom's, so she quickly packed, and we drove the 45 minutes to her mother's house in Sun City Center to drop her off. On the way there we spoke of the realities of me not being there for her. I was crushed, but her pain was far worse. She was stoic and strong. She barely shed a tear. In fact, I cried more than her.

I quietly thought to myself what would happen if I saw her mother while dropping Teri off? Her mother was driving home from the hospital, so there was a remote chance.

It was then that I had one of the worst experiences of my life. As we pulled into the driveway her mother was getting out of her car. Teri got out quickly and went over to her and they hugged. I knew the feeling they were experiencing as I went through losing my parents. I sat in the car quietly giving them their moment. I quietly got out and took out Teri's luggage and left it for her in the driveway. I got back in the car and backed out of the driveway. My lasting image will always be of her Mom, who I have known and loved for 25 years, completely ignoring me. She never looked my way. There is no way for anyone to know the emotional pain I was feeling unless they have felt the pain of being rejected simply because you are being who you want to be. I began to cry. My crying quickly turned to uncontrollable sobbing. All kinds of thoughts raced through my brain.

"Was my decision to come out as trans a big mistake?"

"Was I being selfish?"

"How could I do this to Teri? How could I have put her in such a vulnerable position?"

"Why am I being so rejected? I loved these people for 25 years and I still love her daughter and she still loves me."

I yelled loudly in the car, "It's just not fair!"

I reached out to my daughter Lindsay on the phone. In between my tears I told her, "I just dropped Teri off to deal with her father's passing. I wasn't welcomed. My heart is breaking." She was compassionate and insightful. When a person needs some advice, she usually is spot on. Her best advice was when she said, "You can't control what other people think." I had heard that same line many times in the years since coming out. I despise hearing it, although it's true and it's my reality.

She further said, "Dad, older people have a hard time with this kind of stuff. You need to get over it." I needed a good slap in the face and I got it. I drove back to Siesta Key, which is certainly not like being sent to Hell, but I still felt terrible about the situation.

Teri spent a couple days with her mother at her house before coming back down to Siesta for the final two days. We enjoyed the beach, some great dinners and listened to some live music. We were trying to make the best of it, but I knew that I would be leaving on Wednesday with Teri staying behind for her father's services over the weekend.

I woke up way too early that Wednesday morning with all kinds of thoughts going through my brain. I packed, dressed and tried to keep my mind busy. At 6:30 AM I woke her and said in tears, "I am here for you in any way I can be. I love you no matter what." I gave her a kiss knowing that I would be leaving her alone to deal with her grief. I couldn't have felt worse. She was there for me every moment of my parents' passing and I couldn't imagine doing it alone, yet I drove away, again shedding tears. Again, I yelled, "It's just not fair," but there was nothing I could do about it. Bringing it up would only reflect on me thinking about myself and not her family.

My ongoing attempt to be accepted by Teri's family continued with little progress. Following the death of her father in November, I decided to not attempt to contact Teri's mother Carol, as it would not be proper, since she was still grieving. In January, I still had not expressed my sorrow over Mike's passing, so I wrote her an email and expressed my true feelings of love for Mike. He was like a second father to me and although we differed on many political subjects, we were still able to move beyond that and have a proper son-in-law father-in-law relationship. He liked to play golf and while he was still able, we would often play the club that he was a member of. I wrote the email knowing full well that she probably would not respond and sure enough I never received any response, as well as to any of the other emails I wrote almost weekly to her for a number of weeks. All of them expressed my love for her and my desire to be part of her life again. I was just always hopeful that maybe one would come back with a positive response.

2018 moved along and in May, Teri and I planned a trip to Mexico. Teri thought a trip to see her mother before would work out logistically. Once again, I was not invited and in subsequent conversations with Teri it became obvious to me that there is no way she would ever accept me, at least in the foreseeable future. I was heartbroken to hear this again and made the decision to just stop trying and caring. I tried to not think about her mother or her brothers and their family, who also had rejected me. I wanted to remove them from my life.

In late June 2018, Teri got a note from her sister-in-law Barbara about having an 80th birthday party for her mother, Carol, in December. I overheard the plans being made and was hoping that perhaps I would be invited. I asked Teri. The answer came back with a resounding, "Cami, that's not going to happen. Give it up." That was coupled with another family function, albeit not a good one, where they would all get together to spread her father Michael's ashes in Florida. That would again require Teri going to Florida. It turns out, I would not be invited to that family event either.

I hit an emotional wall and felt a strong desire to write her mother, brothers and sisters-in-law expressing to them my disappointment. I wrote them without telling Teri, which was, in retrospect, a bad idea. I "begged" them to allow me back into the family. It was a heartfelt letter and certainly not written on the cuff. I gave a lot of time and thought as to what I would say. Well, I didn't hear from them for a week, so I sent another note saying, "Any answer would be better than no answer." Well, that got my sister-in-law Barb to call me, who started off by criticizing me and wordsmithing my letter. I had said in it, "If you truly love your daughter and or sister, then if nothing more please reconsider for her sake." They took that as meaning that her mother or brothers didn't really love her, which is obviously not what I intended. I was trying to make a point, but it didn't come across that way. I should have said, "If you want to show some EXTRA love for your daughter or sister...."

This issue became the only subject brought up during the heated call and my request was never even addressed. I was mad, upset and hurt again. Afterwards, Teri had a difficult conversation with her mother and sister-in-law Barbara. She then told me, "Cami, you just need to move on as this is never going to happen." I gave it a lot of thought and as difficult as it is, I have done just that. It saddens me deeply that her mother may possibly die in the upcoming years and that I will not have been able to tell her one more time that I love her, but that is her decision, not mine. I must live with it, just as I have had to live with many other close friendships that have ended because of my transition. I have talked to many friends about these breakups in trying to understand why. I still search for an answer I can live with. I'd like to believe that time will perhaps change their minds and ease mine, so I remain hopeful. I know who I am and what makes me happy and that is me being Cami. If they don't like it, it's their loss.

Chapter 28

One funny occurrence happened when I first came out. I was in the Sprint store getting a rebate issue resolved. I was waiting patiently while the salesman was on the phone trying to help me when a young woman walked in. She was in a complete panic because her phone had died, and she was yelling, "I'm on call for work. I need my phone." She jumped right in and started telling the salesman what phone she needed when he said, "Well, I do have this other person (that being me) that I'm helping right now," but as I looked at her and saw the panic on her face, I said, "Please, take care of her, she seems like she needs help more then I." So, he goes out back to get her the new phone and she says to me, "Why is it that phones always break down for no reason?" I said, "Well, there is always a reason" and I proceeded to tell her about the time mine broke "for no reason."

I was at Viva Wild Side in Las Vegas in 2016 and we all were out one-night club dancing in the downtown area. I had put my phone in-between my boobs, so it was with me. Little did I realize; I was sweating profusely the entire night. I had started hormones and one relatively quick thing that occurred was that my boobs had increased in size and that coupled with breast forms allowed me to present a nice breast appearance. I was also seeing other subtle changes from the hormones, such as body hair loss, a general feeling of calmness and a softening of personality from the strong male figure I was as Tom. I liked what was happening.

Well, the next morning, I woke up and my phone was dead. I didn't understand why, so I went to the Sprint store where a technician looked at it and said, "It has water damage." I said, "It hasn't even been near water." He then asked, "What did you do last night?" I then said, "Well, I was out dancing. I had the phone in-between my boobs..." I immediately stopped in mid-sentence as I realized that in putting my phone between my sweaty boobs that's how the water damage occurred. He laughed and looked at me and said, "I have heard a lot of crazy reasons, but never heard of that reason for having water damage." Not sure if this was something I should be proud of, but I jokingly replied, "Something tells me that I am probably the first transgender women to do it."

The woman gasped when she heard my story. She looked at me and emphatically says, "Oh my God!" I said, "Oh my God what?" She then said, "I was out hiking today, and I put my phone between my boobs. I was sweating a lot, so the phone got wet and that's probably why the phone isn't working." We all laughed and laughed over what was obviously a crazy coincidence. Especially because the Sprint salesman said he had never seen or heard of it happening before or that way either.

Obviously, we had bonded and became part of an exclusive club, "The Sweaty Boob Damaged Phone Club."

Chapter 29

Although I have seen plenty of rejection, I also have found amazing acceptance and love from complete strangers. Many times, I have been approached at stores, concerts or walking about and have had people come up to me and say they wanted to meet me and that they wanted to understand more about me and being transgender. Typically, these are people that have had little contact with someone who's transgender, so they are curious, and they want to understand more. I've always been willing to take whatever time is needed to do so. Believe me I also get my share of crazy looks. I love walking by couples, typically older and Mormon, who I know have noticed me, for example in a mall and after I pass them, I turn around knowing that they will look back at me and when they do I just wave. It's hysterical to watch them react to the fact that they have been caught. But that's OK. If I wasn't out and about, they would not have seen me, and they would not have been exposed to a transgender person. Ultimately, that is the best I can hope to achieve with people that I don't know.

I feel very blessed to have come out in the Park City/Summit County area. It is a very liberal county in a state known for being very conservative and Mormon, whose beliefs are routed in being anti LGBTQ. Yet, the people of Park City are open, progressive and very accepting. There is very little if any crime and the biggest offensive thing someone could do is to say, "I hate skiing." From the moment I came out, thanks to the wonderful story written about me in the local paper the Park Record, I have been amazingly accepted by the community. I continued to play in the Men's golf league at Park City and never heard any negative feedback or comments. I am often asked why I don't play in the women's league, but I think since I have the choice, I would rather be competitive against the men as some women may not think it's fair to them and I would agree, as I am a low handicapper.

I am welcomed everywhere, and in many cases, locals are excited that I am out and about and, in their businesses, or at events. More than once, I have been asked if I am Caitlyn Jenner. Although a crazy question, I would be lying if I didn't say it was flattering as she was instrumental in me coming out when I did.

Often, I shop at Smith's supermarket and people I know, or even total strangers have come up to me. They have said things like, "I have seen you around town and I wanted to tell you how much I admire you and the courage you have shown," or a simple, "Looking good Cami." Or, "Love you Cami." Rarely, is my old name of Tom even spoken anymore. I have seen genuine warmness and acceptance from so many people on countless occasions. Summers in Park City are loaded with a busy concert schedule and Teri and I go often. I am always the social butterfly, chatting with friends or strangers, dancing and singing along with the band and have no inhibitions about being Cami in front of thousands and none of them to seem to care either.

Amazingly, in my small little western hometown of Kamas, which is predominantly Mormon and where the old timers are farmers or ranchers, I have seen no push back or animosity. In the grocery store I am warmly greeted by the workers and locals. Trust me, I get plenty of looks of disbelief, but no offensive comments are ever spoken directly to me. On my daily morning walks with Jeter (and sometimes a handful of other neighborhood dogs) I am greeted warmly when I see others on a walk. One woman, who drove past me often, stopped one day and said, "I see you daily on your walk and I've always wanted to tell you how much I admire you. Your courage is inspiring." When I hear things like that it really makes me feel good. It's the kind of positive feedback all transgender people need and desire.

I recall once when one mother I didn't know came up to me at the supermarket and said, "You are an inspiration to me and my family. I have a transgender daughter, male to female, and whenever I see you, I tell her how out and about you are. Would you mind taking the time to talk to her?" "Off course I will," I responded. I called her and her daughter later that day and we wound up having a long chat on the phone that I believe helped them both and gave her more courage in her journey.

I was fortunate to speak to the GSA group at Park City High School in late 2016. It was a great experience for me, and I believe for the students. In seeing someone as old as me come out at 63 years old that them coming out at a young age gives them hope for a long and bright future living as their true self. I encouraged them to make this decision with help from family and if needed a therapist. As they listened to my story of hiding behind my secret for 58 years, they couldn't believe it and asked, "How could you wait so long?" I told them, "Things were different growing up in the 60's, 70's and 80's. Dressing as a woman was looked at as being strange and perverse and the constant fear of being outed was a huge fear factor for me." I further explained, "There was no internet to go to and quickly read about these things. All that changed in the late 90's, so it was then that I educated myself on what I was going through." Knowledge gave me confidence, which many of these kids already have. I am slightly envious that they still have their whole life ahead of them. I was received with much appreciation and I look forward to more of these opportunities.

I once had an interesting encounter at the Canyons golf course where I work part time. I had brought a couple in from the parking lot on the shuttle. They were from Palm Springs, a very liberal community with a huge LGBTQ population.

We were chatting on the way into the course and as the man was getting out, he answered one of my questions with a "Yes sir." Well, I get mis-gendered many times in my job there, but to me it comes with being out as a transwoman in public. It never bothers me as my voice is a dead giveaway, which I don't try to hide or mask, but his comment must have bothered him, because when they got to the area where they take off in their golf-cart he came up to me and in front of many others said, "Cami, I am truly sorry for mis-gendering you earlier. I live in Palm Springs and I see gays, lesbians and trans people all the time. I am very accepting, and I apologize for misspeaking." I was floored that he would apologize, as it certainly wasn't necessary, but at the same time it was very welcomed. He was a real gentleman and very vulnerable, and I thanked him for saying that.

At the end of their round when they were dropping off the cart, he flipped me a $20 tip. I said, "Really, that isn't necessary," knowing full well he was trying to make up for his mistake, but he insisted I take it. We pool our tips, so it wasn't going in my pocket anyway, but the gesture was very appreciated. I was embarrassed knowing that my co-workers had witnessed all of it.

Some people's conscience works in strange ways and I often wonder after someone mis-genders me, mostly men, if on second thought they don't question what they said. After all, how many 'guys' have boobs, long blond hair, wear a skirt, lipstick and makeup. All I need to remember is I was once one of them and how oblivious men can be. Sorry guys, just saying… or should I say, "Pay attention."

The most significant acceptance by anyone has been from my amazing wife, Teri. Her unconditional love for me is so inspiring. I could only wish she could talk to more women who are in the same position as her, as I believe she could help many others. She has been challenged by her mother and family to justify how she could still want to be with me. She defends me and her position without hesitation or regret. I love her for that and hope we will remain together until death do us part.

So, what has it been like since I went 24/7? Things have certainly changed. I don't dress like I am going out to the debutant ball. I've become the typical female in appearance. My hair grew out and most of the time I go without a wig. If I can get away with no makeup or less, I do. However, I always look forward to going out and about and presenting myself as Cami. I don't have any reservations or fears and my only hope is that by people encountering me day in and out, they will become more understanding and accepting. I have had feelings of sadness in knowing that I have lost friends and I have had to deal with being lonely more so than ever before in my life. For me, that's not easy as I've always been a very social and outgoing person. I'm still learning to cope and hoping that things will change, but in the meantime, I will persevere.

Every day I try to live to my personal mission statement and to be a good person while on this wonderful earth. When I feel it happening, and it happens often, I realize it's all worth it. So far, so good. I look forward to my next 66 years.

Chapter 30

Back in 2010 I was spending a lot of time on the internet looking for information on crossdressing and transgenderism. I came across a website called Diva Las Vegas. I was curious as it stated it was not a convention, more of an outing. It looked like fun, but I had rarely ventured out of the house dressed. The thought of it scared the hell out of me. I talked to Teri about going and she said yes. I could not wait for the week to come. I packed more stuff then I could possibly wear in a month.

It turned out to be an exciting week. I met lots of people with similar stories. I had a blast. I attended events, ate dinners with strangers and danced and drank until the wee hours. I had found a community that I was immediately welcomed into. I met girls who would become life-long friends.

The way it works is that some attendees organize an event and through the website attendees can sign up to go to that event. It requires some volunteering, so the next year I jumped in with both feet and ran a couple events. Year after year I would attend and got more involved in planning events. One year I won the prize for most hospitable and welcoming attendee. Over 150 people attended so it was a big honor for me. After years of being one of the most active attendees I was appointed as one of three national organizers. It is one of the largest transgender/cross-dresser's outings in the country and I am proud to help in it happening each year.

People attend from all over the country and from overseas. It gives me huge satisfaction to organize events and see the joy that many of these cross-dressers or trans people get from participating. Like my first DLV in 2010, it is the first time many girls have been out in public. They come to Vegas scared to death and they leave with unbelievable confidence. I enjoy helping my trans community grow through Diva Las Vegas.

Over the years, my trans girlfriends and I have had some incredible experiences. Most of them involve things like dining out at a great restaurant, doing tourist things, golfing, gambling, drinking, partying and dancing, but each year my takeaway is the friendships I created that have become lifetime.

One year, I organized an event that included going to see the Donny and Marie Show at the Flamingo, which was just fantastic and very entertaining. Following the show, I had made a reservation for all 20 of us to go to dinner at a great steakhouse in the casino. We were all seated together in the back of the restaurant. I was seated in the middle looking out into the restaurant. I noticed a familiar looking man approaching us. I was shocked when I realized ~~that~~ Donnie Osmond was coming towards our table looking like he was going to speak with us.

He came up and asked, "How are you ladies this evening? I noticed you at the show. Did you like it?" Someone replied that it was great. He then took the time to talk to each of us. I knew he lived in Provo, which is very close to where I live in Utah, so I mentioned that I was from Park City. He immediately jumped into a conversation with me and we hit it off. He was a gentleman. It was a thrill for all of us.

We have had some late, late night drunken forays over the years. One night a fight broke out after some foreigners made some crude comments about us while we were sitting at a bar. Some other straight guys nearby overheard it and didn't like what they said and came to our assistance, even though we didn't ask for it. It was a chaotic scene for a few moments until 5 security guards came in and broke it up. We never even left our bar seat and it was interesting to watch. It was nice to be defended and made us feel like true women.

Vegas has always been a SAFE place for us to go, stay and vacation. We are welcomed with open arms at the local bars where many of us have become regulars. Carnival Court, an outdoor bar located between The LINQ and Harrah's, was one of our favorites. A great 80's band called the Whip Its played weekend days and by adding in some great, fun flair bartenders made day drinking a must do. We all loved to dance and brought lots of energy to the crowd, who were fascinated by a bunch of trans women who liked to have fun. Many quickly joined us on the dance floor and bought us drinks. I had no fear of being out in front of others and showing my true self. Diva Las Vegas gave me the confidence to be bold and sassy.

I love the feeling I get when I see a "newbie" come out of her shell for the first time. I remember more than once walking out of a first-timers room, down the elevator and helping that person walk through the casino for the first time. Watching fear become confidence is simply addictive. I love that each year I can help transwomen have a special time in their lives. To some, it is everything.

Chapter 31

Just after the stunning election results of 2016, I kept hearing about an upcoming Women's March that was to occur in mid-January 2017. Social media was abuzz about how women throughout the country would be marching for women's rights and their outrage at Donald Trump. Liberal women (and men) were aghast. They felt abused, insulted and wanted to take to the streets.

I felt the same, so I decided to go and participate. The last protest I actively marched in was some 40 years earlier over a mining companies blasting of rock that was impacting my home. Quite the dichotomy.

I woke up that Saturday to a snowy morning and although 12 inches of fresh, light powder was beckoning me to go ski Deer Valley Ski Resort, I opted out, which was the first sign that I was in for an amazing morning. I had made my sign the night before. It read TRANS LIVES MATTER in big, colorful letters. The police had estimated that perhaps 2,000-3,000 people would attend, which by Park City standards was a no brainer to handle, after all, the 4th of July parade brought out 20,000 people. Well, no one gave a lot of thought to the news of upcoming snow, the fact that the ski resorts would be humming on a Saturday morning and that the Sundance Film Festival had just started on Thursday. The town was bursting with people and many wanted to be a part of what has now become an historical event not only in Park City, but the United States and the world.

I dodged a bullet with my travel into Park City as I just missed the roads becoming slow and unpassable. The local radio station was reporting huge traffic issues, especially on I-80 coming up from Salt Lake. I parked in the lower Deer Valley lot and waited for a bus, which wasn't coming, so for the first time in 45 years, I nervously stuck my finger out to hitch a ride. I didn't give a lot of thought to being trans as I was in a pink jacket and so bundled up in winter clothes no one could tell anyway. Sure enough, a guy in a beautiful Audi Sedan pulled up to give me a ride. I got in and noticed he was an Uber driver. I offered to pay, but he said, "No way. I picked you up as a favor." He dropped me off as close as he could to Main Street even going out of his way. The day was starting off well.

I stopped at Flanagan's Bar on Main Street as they were hosting early AM coffee and pastries. It was packed, and it was then that I realized this was going to be an amazing rally regardless of the weather.

I made my way up to the starting area at the Wasatch Brewery parking lot with my Trans Lives Matter poster. TV cameras and radio stations were broadcasting live, and I was interviewed a couple times. I handled it well. Obviously, being a trans woman was appealing to the media. I saw some old friends and made lots of new ones. I felt amazing love and acceptance from everyone there. The crowd was bursting at the seams. Many wore pink knitted caps known as "pussy hats" in protest of Trump's past comments about women. It was snowing hard, but the energy level was electric. I said to myself, "There are a lot of people here. This is awesome!"

Slowly, the march began, and I joined in and found myself intoxicated by the various chants, the cheering by the spectators and the support from everyone there. To my knowledge, I was the only transgender person who marched out of the 8,000 that did so on that cold, blustery, snowy morning.

When people saw me and my sign they cheered mightily. People who knew me yelled, "Way to go Cami, we love you!" Others gave me high fives, big smiles or a thumb up. I was thrilled to be representing the trans community in my hometown. Down Main Street we marched in a sloppy, dirty, slushy mess and headed to the City Parking lot for a rally and speeches. Among the speakers were standup comedienne Jessica Williams, filmmaker Kimberly Peirce and television personality Chelsea Handler. All of whom were inspirational, moving and their words timely. The crowd was fired up.

When it ended, I felt an amazing sense of accomplishment. I was a trans woman marching in the Women's march and I did so proudly. I felt strongly that I needed to be more of a visible advocate for the trans community and I was doing just that.

The adrenalin to do more was calling. I knew that I could make a bigger difference than I already was. But I kept asking myself, "What else could I do?" When I first came out, I had set as my personal mission statement:

I want to change people's perception of the trans community by being a true advocate. Although I want to change the world's perception, I have come to realize that I can only do that one person at a time. When I meet someone, I want to leave them with a good impression of me and my community. I will answer all questions or concerns with confidence, honesty and integrity.

I do my best to live to this mission every day of my life. It is always on my mind. When I am able to accomplish it, in even the smallest of ways, I feel good that I am making a difference.

One answer to how I could do more was social media. Over the years I became a big social media user, primarily Facebook, but more and more on Instagram as well. When Cami was in hiding, I had a second Facebook account under my alias Cami Desiree. My friends list consisted primarily of people in the cross dressing or transgender communities. I was always afraid I would out myself somehow on my regular Facebook account and eventually I did, but luckily to only one friend, who I immediately told the truth to and asked for his confidentiality. When I came out 24/7, I closed my old Cami Desiree Facebook, but only after telling those friends to transfer to my original Tom Richardson account, which I was renaming Cami Richardson.

I am not shy about being a trans advocate on social media and often post my thoughts, opinions and often inspirational messages about being trans. It gives me an outlet to have a voice and I believe my Facebook friends appreciate me doing so. Following Trump's election, I was a very vocal opponent and often would comment on his actions, comments and pure stupidity. I love the feedback and comments I get and hope that friends are becoming more accepting of the transgender community by my example.

In 2019, I was asked to become a member of an advisory committee promoting Social Equity in the Park City community. I represent the transgender community and I am proud to be able to help achieve equality in our community for all. We deserve to live our lives the way we want and to be the people we want to be and to do so in a welcoming environment.

Chapter 32

The question as to how I could do more advocacy was answered when fate would come into play. In November 2017, I had been in retirement for over 10 months and was getting bored. I was writing this book, skiing and golfing, but I needed more, I wanted to be productive, so I went to the most obvious places to get a job, which were the Park City ski resorts. I dusted off my resume and humbly went and applied. I really wasn't concerned about prejudice against me being trans as these are big companies that must follow non-discriminatory hiring practices. I had a great interview at Deer Valley Ski Resort and was offered a position working with kids in the ski school. It was intriguing but didn't feel right.

I applied to Park City Mountain Resort in the hopes that I could work at Canyons Village, as 20 years earlier as CFO of American Ski Company, I helped purchase that side of the resort, then known as Wolf Mountain. It had been my home ski resort for 20 years. I got a call from a recruiter for Vail Resorts for a phone interview. I didn't see how I could adequately tell my story over the phone, but I wound up with a great recruiter, who had read my resume, which included my ski resort experience. Apprehensively, I told her about me being trans. She could not have cared less. She listened, and we talked about opportunities.

After 30 minutes, she said, "Cami, I have never had such a great interview with a candidate. You are more than qualified. I have the authority to hire someone on the spot, but I have never done it. But there is always a first, so would you come to work for us as a Greeter at Canyons Village?"

I was taken back as I didn't expect an offer so quickly. I awkwardly said, "Sure. How much per hour?"

She replied, "Well, what is your salary expectation?"

I jokingly said, "Well, I normally make $75 to $100 per hour."

She replied, "How about $11 per hour and a ski pass?"

I said, "Sure. I'm in."

I hung up and my first reaction was thinking, only $11 per hour? I rationalized that the hourly rate doesn't include the value of the ski pass I would get and which I had already bought that I would get a refund on and that Teri could get a dependent pass, both of which are worth almost $2,000. Other than standing out in the cold weather it wasn't going to be that difficult a job. I would be greeting and assisting skiers with their questions and needs.

I reported to work the second day the resort opened for the year. It was a sunny, warm day in the 40's. It had been 20 years since I had been an employee at a resort, although now this was an entry level position. I was tickled pink not only to be working and to be productive, but because I believe my personal mission statement to improve the world's perception of the trans community, would be accomplishable and just as I previously said, one person at a time.

I would meet hundreds of people each day. I was one of the first staff members they would see when they got to the Forum where the ticket booths and lifts are located. I can safely assume that many of these people have never met a transgender person. My actions would dictate their first impression, not only of me, but the trans community. What a fantastic opportunity it was for me to shine. It turned out I had landed in the perfect spot, without it even being the goal. I would be an advocate for the LGBTQ community by just being me.

This belief was confirmed when my brother Jim sent me an unsolicited note after he heard the job news that read, "This is your calling, Cami. This is bigger than being a CFO, firefighter, inn owner, director or store owner. This is more than selfies on Facebook or having fun with trans friends in Vegas (who already know the ups and downs). God put you out there making $11 an hour to help people understand. This is your opportunity to help change the world! Stay warm, show up on time and smile!" Better words were never written and true. I was living my mission statement!

The season went on and I was truly happy in my minor role as Greeter, but major role as an ambassador to the trans community.

I had a couple great experiences that winter. One afternoon a woman stopped me while walking the hallway at the Park City Hospital.

She asked, "Are you Cami?"

I turned and said, "Yes, I am."

She then said, "I was at the Canyons last month and out of the clear blue, you came up to me and asked if I needed any help. I have to say you were very helpful. It was surprising to me that someone would do that."

I said, "Well, thank you, it's nice to get good feedback."

She then said, "You are representing yourself and your community well. I admire you. Keep it up." I was happy to hear that.

On my last day of work in April 2018 I noticed a mother and her young child approaching. It was such a cute picture as the mother was helping the girl to walk holding her hand and keeping her up. I couldn't help myself and said, "Hello." The mother responded back, "Hi there." I told her that her daughter was very cute and asked, "How old is she?" She replied, "She's 18 months." We went back and forth for a while and I learned they were from South Carolina, a conservative state. As the conversation was ending, I said, "So, when your daughter gets older you can tell her she met her first transgender person at 18 months." The mother, who was in her 30's said, "Well, I just did as well." I was surprised and said, "Well, I hope I left a good impression on you." She said, "Most definitely. It was a pleasure to meet you."

When my shift was over, I got in my car to drive home. I thought back on that encounter and how my goal that winter in doing this job was to be visible as a trans woman, represent my community well and leave people with a good impression. Was it just ironic or fate that this encounter happened that last day, so that I could walk away knowing I had met my goals? I was so happy and proud and thought to myself, "I can only enlighten one person at a time and I just did." I was so happy that I cried real tears.

I always questioned how I could measure how successful I had been in life, without being too biased. Based on all my accomplishments, I always believed I was successful. After all, I had a great family, I had rescued people, delivered babies, took a company public and started successful businesses. I was so wrong. Those weren't accomplishments but rather milestones on a path to true success. I thought back to my college years and of reading about Maslow's hierarchy of needs. I always questioned if I could reach the top of the pyramid, known as *Self-actualization*. This level of need refers to what a person's full potential is and the realization of that potential. It is the desire to accomplish everything that one can, to become the most that one can be. I always thought to get there I would have to be powerful man and super wealthy, and to be philanthropic. Now I wondered, could I get there by simply being inspirational? Could I be a giver and not a taker and find true happiness?

Turns out I had found the perfect place to be in my life at 64 years old and after 58 other jobs. My life had all fallen into place. My true success and finding self-actualization came from being a Greeter making $11 an hour and being out in public as a proud transwoman and living my personal mission.

I was good friends with the Golf Pro at Canyons Golf resort and over the course of the winter we would run into one another. I asked him what he thought about me working at the course that summer. He thought I would be a great fit, so he hired me. As player service rep, I had to move golf carts out in the morning, marshal the course, shuttle the guests to and from the parking lot, load bags unto golf carts and wash the carts at shifts end. Bottom line, it was hard work and something I wasn't used to. But I persevered and kept busy. I enjoyed the work and got to play free golf at the course.

Most importantly, I got the opportunity to present myself as a transwoman and interact with the golfers. I had come a long way from when I was a golfer in my male mode. I often could see their reaction to me, which mostly was bewilderment. It's funny how some men just don't know how to react. I could see them pointing me out to their friends and when driving away getting a good laugh. It didn't bother me as my feeling was that they had just been exposed to a transwoman, possibly for the first time, and that's exactly what my mission is, whether it was a good or bad reaction. I also am so comfortable in my own skin at this point and since I don't present myself badly, I'm not embarrassing myself, but rather they are embarrassing themselves.

As I entered the winter of 2018-19, I went back to work as a greeter at the ticket booth at Canyons Village, a part of Park City Mountain Resort. I was healthy after a long period of fighting off a shoulder injury and coming off a nice long vacation in Marco Island, Florida with Teri. I received a big raise of $0.11 and was now making $12.36 per hour after Vail Resorts raised the minimum wage to $12.25/hour. I often think about what I used to make as an executive in the ski industry and laugh, but I wasn't there for the money, I was there to continue my mission on a daily basis of enlightening people about the transgender community.

The season went along in a fairly uneventful manner, but I did have a few interesting interactions with guests that left lasting memories.

One day, I was helping two guys, who had their 12-year-old sons with them on a ski trip. They were from the New York area and I engaged with them easily. We talked Yankee baseball, and all was good with the world. I said goodbye but ran into them later on at the Umbrella Bar having lunch, about two hours later. I asked, "How were your ski runs?" One guy replied, "We still haven't been out yet. These kids are driving us crazy."

I had left my greeting job and was conducting some surveys for Ski Utah, which is another part-time job I had, so I asked them if they wanted to take a survey.

Normally, I give the survey to the individual to complete themselves, but since they were dealing with their kids, I started to ask them questions to which they were replying. I got curious and asked, "Are you guys just here for skiing?" One guy replied, "No, I actually had a speaking engagement yesterday down in Las Vegas." I found that interesting and asked him, "What do you speak about?" He replied thoughtfully and said, "Well, I am a brain cancer survivor and I have written a book about my experience and that of my father-in-law, who came down with cancer at the same time. Unfortunately, he did not survive, and my talk is about how I overcame these challenges. In fact, I've actually written a book about it and have now done 38 speaking engagements, including a TED Talk."

I was impressed and my eyes lit up as I was in the process of completing this book. I told him what it was about, and he thought it sounded interesting and offered his help. He also had self-published his memoir and it has become a best-seller, so it gave me reason to hope. We exchanged contact information and in doing more research on him he is quite simply an amazing individual. One of the great joys in this job is the people you meet and engage with. He was one of them and one I will never forget.

My next encounter was with an older man, whom I was helping as he was standing at the ticket window waiting for a seller. When the seller came over, he actually thanked me and gendered me as a female, which left me feeling somewhat good. Upon getting his ski ticket he came back to get his skis and I was nearby. I asked him if he was all set. He looked inquisitively at me and said, "Are you a male or a female? I replied, "Well, I am actually transgender." He paused and said pointedly, "Oh, you can't be transgender as you have X chromosomes." He said it very sternly and I realized that his take on me had changed completely. I simply looked at him and said, "Well, you can think what you want, but so can I and I'm transgender." I then walked away thinking that I just can't change everyone's perception of the trans community, and he is entitled to his, even though I believe it's wrong.

On Fat Tuesday during Mardi Gras week, I was working the morning shift and the ticket staff wanted to celebrate Mardi Gras, so we decorated the ticket booth. We all wore purple and gold beads.

Once again, I wound up helping two guys at the window answering some of their questions until the seller came. Once she started to help them, I walked away but found myself back within earshot of them within a few minutes. One of the guys taps me on the shoulder and looks at me and says, "By the way, your costume today is really good. You look just like a woman." It was kind of a backhanded compliment, but I looked at the guy and said, "I'm going to take that as a compliment as I'm actually transgender." He laughed and said, "Seriously?" I nodded and we both had a good laugh of it.

The winter progressed and the snow kept falling, resulting in a record snowfall year. We had excellent ski conditions throughout the whole ski-season, and I wound up skiing 65 days for a total of 1,003,000 vertical feet for the season. At 65 years old, I was proud that I could stay healthy and have such a great season. I skied at 12 of the best ski resorts in the U.S., including my first family ski trip to Jackson Hole, Wyoming, which is often voted the top ski resort in North America. It lived up to its expectations and my family and I had a great ski weekend topped off by a weekend of concerts by top bands during the Rendezvous Festival, including Nathaniel Rateliff and the Night Sweats and Grace Potter.

In late January I experienced a good karma kind of day. I was able to ski first thing in the morning at Park City Village on a crisp, blue bird, groomer day and the skiing was fantastic. While skiing I signed up for the Sundance Film Festival waitlist to try and see a new movie called *Adam* which was promoted as an LGBT movie although it would turn out to be mostly about trans people.

I left the resort at 11 AM and walked down to the Library Theatre. As I stood in line, I was hopeful that I'd get into the movie as I was assigned number 26, but it's never guaranteed. Sure enough, the admittance line cut off with me being the next person to get in. I was feeling disappointed when out of thin air an unknown woman came up to me and handed me a free ticket and said, "You need to go see this movie." I was shocked and thankful and offered her the $20 bill I had in my hand for the ticket, but she would not take it.

The movie was very inspiring, and I hope it gets picked up so the general population can see it. It is set in New York City in 2006 and speaks to the challenges trans and gay people face just trying to live their lives. During the Q&A at the end, I felt the need to comment and stood up and gave a pro trans speech and was surprised when the entire audience cheered for my comments. I met the cast and felt such a camaraderie with them. It was a day I will never forget. I took pictures with the director and actors as well as the writer. I left feeling lots of love for the transgender community. I love Sundance and all it offers to Park City and the world!

In December 2018, Teri and I were having morning coffee when she turned to me and out of the clear blue said, "I've been giving this some thought and if you really want to get boobs then you should just get them." I was dumbfounded and asked, "Really, are you sure you're okay with that?" She said, "Yeah, go for it." I was ecstatic as I had not brought it up with her to discuss for a good year and a half and at that time as she wasn't in favor of it, in fact, she was emphatic about it. I always tried to be cognizant of Teri's feelings about me transitioning, specifically undergoing surgeries. I really wanted to get boobs at a minimum, but since she didn't, I had to let it go. So, when she said go ahead, I was cautiously afraid she would change her mind, so I tried to not be too obviously happy, but deep down I was.

I then proceeded to do some homework and found out that our health insurance would cover breast augmentation for transgender women and in many cases not for cisgender females, which I thought was strange. However, I would need a letter from my doctor assessing my condition and diagnosing me as being transgender.

After an initial consultation with a wonderful plastic surgeon in Salt Lake City named Dr. Reuben, I scheduled the surgery for April 11th a few days after I returned from Diva Las Vegas and following the ski season. He had performed breast augmentation on transwomen before, so I felt comfortable using him. As the day for surgery approached, I was excited for what was to come. I opted for a C-D cup in size, which was what I was used to wearing in breast-forms. I came out of the operation fine although the pain was way worse than what I expected. The first opportunity I had when home to take the bandage and bra off and see what I had received, I was thrilled beyond belief. They were beautiful and I felt more complete as a woman. I never imagined this day would occur and was thankful to have such an amazingly accepting spouse in Teri, who gave me the gift of boobs when I least expected it.

In May we took a vacation to Siesta Key, Florida and I was proudly showing them off in my new bathing suits. At one-point while sitting on the beach Teri remarked, "You're going to wind up with tan lines on your boobs if you don't cover them up." I replied, "Yeah, I know. I have been waiting to do exactly that and see tan lines on my boobs for most of my life." She just shook her head.

Chapter 33

In February 2016, when I first came out to my daughter Lindsay and her husband Michael, they were uncomfortable with telling my two grandchildren, Marisa, who was 7 at the time and Patrick, who was 5 at the time. I was disappointed, but their logic was undisputable. In their mind, they were a little too young to completely understand what being transgender means, especially their grandpa being trans. I would have to wait a little longer. Since I didn't have any immediate plans to visit with them, I didn't have to be concerned about being Tom around them. I was hoping it would be sooner than later and just had to respect their decision. Months turned into a year and I began to wonder when they would tell them. I feared having to go back to Tom mode when I saw them. It was agony. Of course, I was of the belief that kids in today's age are very acceptable and articles I read agreed that telling them at a young age should not be considered a problem, but I wasn't going to win that battle.

Teri and I were planning to go back to the east coast in July 2017 for vacation on Cape Cod, which would normally include Lindsay and family joining us at a house rental. I had no desire in back tracking as I had been Cami 24/7 for almost 2 years. I was hoping that they would tell them before the trip.

We happened to be in Florida in May when Lindsay called me. Her first words were, "So we told the kids about Cami." I almost fainted in excitement. I said, "Really?" She said, "Yes and they are fine with it. In fact, they said a kid on the bus they ride was transgender." I thanked her and Michael for taking this big step. It's not easy for parents to have to tell their kids that their grandpa, who they knew as a man was going to be a woman. I think one of the biggest mistakes trans people make is that we don't fully understand the emotional impact our decision to transition has on family members. We just want immediate acceptance and we have an expectation that all of this will be fine.

I was so happy the wait was over, but I still had to go through the realities of meeting them for the first time. I worried about what they would think, although Lindsay had shown them pictures of me as Cami, so they kind of knew what to expect I would look like. Our vacation in July would be the first time I would see them and as the date approached, I was getting anxious. What should I wear? What should I say to them to break the ice? How would they react?

The big day had arrived, and Teri and I were waiting at our nice rental in Falmouth for them to come down from their house in Sudbury. I met them outside as they got out of the car. I gave them both hugs and a kiss and very sheepishly they gave me a hug back. This was difficult as I could see they were apprehensive. They were staring at me trying to take it all in.

We came into the house and I tried to break the tension by saying, "Well, how do you like Cami so far?" They smiled and I said, "I'm the same person I was as grandpa, so just relax and you'll get used to it." As the day went on, we went to the beach where we could relax and have some fun. They could see that I was just like I use to be, and a new level of comfort became the norm. We came back to the house and played some yard games. I had a conversation with Marisa at one point and talked about me being trans. I asked her, "How do you feel about me coming out as trans?" She said, "I'm fine with it, but why did you want to do this?" At 8 years old she was naturally inquisitive. I told her, "Well, I've been having these feelings of wanting to be a woman for a long time. It's hard to explain why but I am living a life that I have always wanted. I hope you will love me as you always have because I still love you very much. I will always be your grandpa, promise." She said, "I know you will." She started to get emotional, so I gave her a big hug and kiss and said, "It will all be fine." We left it at that, and I think the talk helped a lot. I was keenly aware that I was potentially emotionally impacting my grandchildren and I didn't want them to be scarred by this experience. I didn't dwell on it and the rest of the vacation turned out well. It was just as it always was between us. Lots of fun with grandpa spoiling them rotten.

In late 2017, I got a call from Lindsay that would change a lot of our lives pretty quickly. She opened with, "Guess what?" I replied, "I don't have a clue." She continued, "Well....., we have decided to quit our jobs, sell the house and move to the Park City area." I was floored. I couldn't believe what I just heard as for years Lindsay would always ask, "When are you guys moving back east so you can be closer to all of us?" My response would always be, "Yeah that not happening. We love living out here. The weather is great, we are close to the ski areas and there is nothing not to like." She always understood and now she would be joining us. I was ecstatic. I would be able to see my daughter, son-in-law and grandkids on a constant basis. Life was already great and getting even better.

In April of 2018 they accomplished the move and arrived in Utah after a wonderful cross-country excursion. They stayed with us for a week or so until they could move into their rental in Midway, Utah only 20 minutes from our house. Marisa and Patrick had easily adapted to me being Cami and we love spending time together. We got into having Sunday dinners at our house with Teri cooking amazing dinners. During summer vacation I would watch the kids one day per week. We went on some fun daily trips to Museums, the Jordanelle Reservoir, the Adventure Parks at

Park City Mountain and the Olympic Park, Mirror Lake for picnics, the South Summit Aquatics center and more. I got to know them better and their respective personalities and at times had to be a disciplinarian, which I am finding hard to do with your grandchildren.

They have adapted well and are good at pronouns and often call me Cami as a result of what happened on December 24, 2018. I took them to TJ Max to buy some Christmas gifts for their parents. Of course, they were using my money despite me telling them to bring their piggybanks money. Off they ran off into the store to buy that perfect gift for Mom and Dad. I was walking around doing some shopping of my own, when I hear them both yelling out loud, "Grandpa, where are you. Grandpa, where are you?" as they ran through the aisles. I was so embarrassed when they ran up to me showing me their potential gifts. For the first time I realized that presenting as Cami and being called Grandpa is somewhat of a dichotomy and cause others to look. I whispered, "How about we call me Cami today and not Grandpa?" They said, "Sure." And they did from that point on with relative ease.

I've learned that young kids are way ahead of where I was at their age. Acceptance of their transgender grandfather was accomplished far easier than many of my friends and family have been able to do.

It gives me hope that inclusion of all genders, sexual identities and races, in the future, will be the norm and not the exception. We have a long way to go, but I can assure you I will be out in the world as a proud transwoman, who sets an example for others to be guided by learning *Who I Once Was and Who I am Now.*

Epilogue

As I look back over all my 66 years, I can easily say that I've lived an active life. It's been filled with ups and downs, fear and triumph, good and bad, success and failure, fun and hard work, laughs and tears, acceptance and rejection, loneliness and love and machismo and femininity. *Experience your life, it's the only one you get.*

I have had some major regrets. Most significant is that over the years I have done things I regret doing that have hurt people I love. I don't like disappointing others and myself and I did just that. To those people, who may not even now what I did to them, I am truly sorry. *Always be a good person.*

I regret not having come out as transgender at a younger age and for hiding it for so long. Although I have had an amazing life, I can only imagine how much different, not necessarily better, it could have been. If you believe that you may be transgender, I hope that this book has given you the confidence to seek the truth about yourself and the confidence to do something about it. *Live your true self!*

I regret that I didn't give more money to charity and non-profits over the years. I think it's because I can be cheap and that embarrasses me. I always looked for a deal or a way to save money. I justified it by feeling I worked hard for my money and to share it was hard for me even though I know the importance of giving. *If you can't give money, volunteer.*

I regret that I didn't serve in the armed services. I will admit that when my draft number came in high I was happy that I didn't have to serve, as Vietnam was in its heyday. Today, I have the utmost respect for those who did and always go out of my way to say, "Thank you for your service."

Always thank a veteran.

I regret that it took me so long to truly appreciate my family. I took them for granted for years. I realized when I came out what love and acceptance is all about. I love them all and always tell them that. It soothes my soul. *Love your family with all your heart.*

I regret I never applied to the show *Survivor* to be a contestant. I went as far as doing the required video, but never sent it in. I always wonder as I watch the show today what kind of player I would have been. I think I would have learned a lot about my personality, which could only have made me a better person. ***Challenge yourself to do more.***

I am thankful for many things. Mostly for an amazing spouse in Teri, who has accepted me unconditionally. I realize that she might someday decide that a trans-woman isn't for her and want out of our marriage. In fairness to her, I've already given her that option. I'll have to emotionally cross that bridge if I get to it. At our age, our needs change and we must adapt to newness and she has done that with me. She is truly my soulmate and I am so thankful for having her in my life and love her unconditionally. ***Cherish those close to you.***

I am thankful for good health in my family. I pray it continues. The fact that I pray is also something to be thankful for. Believing in a higher power gives me hope. When I need a friend, I always have someone to talk to. ***Talk to God, he'll listen.***

I am excited to be an advocate for the transgender community and you can be as well. You don't have to be LGBTQ+ to be an advocate, so go to your pride parades and speak up if you hear negative comments. ***Be involved, do good.***

I have discovered that happiness in one's life comes from a belief in one's self to be all that one can be. I am doing that every day. ***Reach for your stars.***

I hope those of you that are cross-dressers or transgender have been inspired by what you have just read. We all face challenges that might seem impossible to move beyond, but yet, you will, because it's what you want. You will face fear, rejection and isolation, but be strong and diligent in your quest to be who *YOU* want to be. ***Trans Lives Matter, especially yours!***

I'm not sure what the future will bring. If the past is any indication, I wouldn't rule anything out. I know one thing for sure is that I will live my life to the fullest and see where the wind takes me. It's been an amazing ride so far. **Please stay tuned...**